CROSS STITCH
FOR
KNITWEAR

CROSS STITCH
FOR
KNITWEAR

80 EMBROIDERY DESIGNS

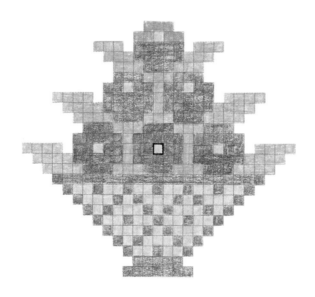

JANET HAIGH

David & Charles

Butterflies, birds and
bees sweater

A DAVID & CHARLES BOOK

Copyright © Janet Haigh 1992
First published 1992

A catalogue record for this book is available from the British Library.

ISBN 0 7153 9929 2

Typeset by ABM Typographics Ltd, Hull
and printed in Italy by Milanostampa SpA
for David & Charles
Brunel House   Newton Abbot   Devon

CONTENTS

INTRODUCTION

Embroidery – especially cross stitch – is currently a highly popular leisure craft. Colourfully decorated knitwear is a highly popular fashion trend. Combine the two and you have an exciting and original approach to both.

All kinds of decoration are explored in this book. It begins with very simple multi-coloured chains, fringes, tassels and bobbles, which can either be used on their own, or as finishing touches to other work. But the emphasis is on cross stitch, from modern pictorial and alphabet designs based on traditional samplers, through bold geometric patterns to nostalgic revivals of the Berlin woolwork that fascinated Victorians for much of the nineteenth century.

Everyone who can embroider a picture or cushion on canvas, following a commercial chart or kit, can produce all these designs; the principle is exactly the same. The difference is that the cross stitch is worked over a special kind of canvas, which is tacked to the knitted surface. When the embroidery is completed, the canvas threads are withdrawn, leaving an evenly worked design on the garment. An added bonus is that there's no tedious filling-in of backgrounds!

Garments for the whole family display a wide range of embroidery (including another Victorian favourite, beading), on sweaters, sweatshirts, jackets, hats, scarves, gloves and socks. The charts can be adapted for other garments; the size of the design itself can be made larger or smaller; and alternative colourways are suggested. Or you can mix and marry different elements of several designs to create an exclusive original of your own.

Buy – or knit – a plain garment. Then set to work with your needle. Some of the embroidery is even easy enough – and great fun – for a child to do. All the designs are so absorbing that an adult will enjoy them to the last stitch – and that satisfying moment when the threads are removed.

BASIC INSTRUCTIONS

CANVAS

The cross stitch embroidery is worked over 'waste canvas', a fine even-weave double-thread canvas, very like those used for needlepoint embroidery. The important difference is that waste canvas is stiffened with a paste that will soften when dampened with water, enabling the threads to be easily pulled apart.

The canvas is tacked to the garment and the stitches are worked through both canvas and the knitted surface beneath. When the embroidery is finished, the threads of the waste canvas are gently withdrawn, leaving the embroidery alone on the backing fabric.

Waste canvas is obtainable from all good craft shops, and comes in various sizes. For the examples shown in the book, four sizes have been used:

14 holes per 2.5cm (1in)
12 holes per 2.5cm (1in)
10 holes per 2.5cm (1in)
8 holes per 2.5cm (1in)

Many of the charts are based on the larger gauges, and to create even stronger and more quickly embroidered designs, some are worked over every other double-thread of the canvas, making the stitches twice the size: eg 8 holes per 2.5cm (1in) worked over every other double-thread = 4 stitches per 2.5cm (1in). This makes large embroideries with even greater impact.

The fewer the number of holes per 2.5cm (1in) of canvas, the larger the embroidery; so, by using a finer gauge of canvas, the embroideries can be reduced in size, making most of the adult designs adaptable for children, and vice versa. The simple calculation which enables you to adapt and re-size any design is explained in the section 'Adapting Designs'.

YARNS

The most suitable yarns to use depend on the fibre of the garment that you are embroidering. Embroidery

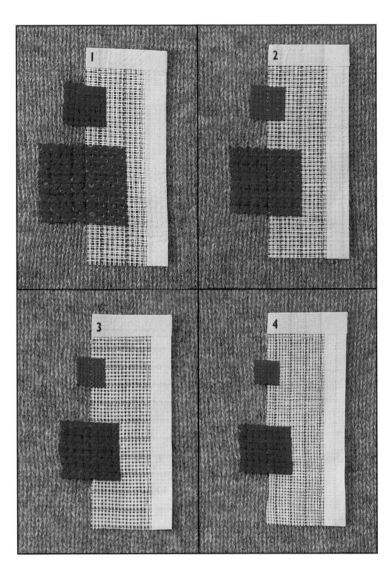

8 x 8 stitch squares of cross stitch worked on the four gauges of canvas: upper squares worked over *every* thread, lower squares worked over every *other* thread

1. 8 holes per 2.5cm (1in); both squares in tapestry wool

2. 10 holes per 2.5cm (1in); upper square using three strands of crewel wool, lower square in tapestry wool

3. 12 holes per 2.5cm (1in); upper square using two strands of crewel wool, lower square in tapestry wool

4. 14 holes per 2.5cm (1in); upper square using two strands of crewel wool, lower square in tapestry wool

wools are the best choice for woollen sweaters, as they are available in a wide range of colours, shading from the palest tints to the darkest tones.

Tapestry wools are available in most craft supply shops and large stores. They are 4-ply yarns making dense fat stitches that fill the embroidered area well, completely covering the ground.

Crewel wools are finer yarns, which can be used singly or in doubles and triples. They are ideal for small woollen embroideries.

Stranded and soft cottons are used on all cotton sweatshirts and cotton knitwear. When working with stranded cottons, always separate all the strands then place them together again before threading your needle; this ensures a neater, plumper stitch. Soft cotton is used for making tassels, fringes and pompons, but stranded cottons may be substituted.

NEEDLES

Tapestry needles are used for the wool embroidery, as they have large eyes to enable you to thread thick yarns, and the blunt ends won't split the knitted fabric. For the finer pieces of embroidery on close-gauge canvas, a pointed crewel needle with a large eye is more convenient, and crewel needles are recommended for all cotton (floss) embroideries on sweatshirts.

Choose a needle with an eye large enough to carry your yarn through the hole it makes in the ground fabric, without having to tug hard to pull it through.

Bodkins can be used for the multiple yarn embroidery.

GARMENTS

This book enables you to turn inexpensive garments, bought from a shop or chain store, into exclusive hand-embroidered designs. But although this is achieved in a short time, with little effort, it is important to take care to select a suitable basic garment. Poor quality knitwear will never look good, and won't provide a suitable (or worthy) background for your handiwork.

Look for predominantly woollen garments: 100% is best, but at least a ratio of 80% wool to 20% other fibres. This is important because wool, unlike man-made fibres, is very forgiving and is easily coaxed back into shape with light steaming and pressing.

Remember that simple, elegant styles are best, as they allow all the attention to focus on the embroidery. Although the designs are most suited to 'T'-shape garments with set-in sleeves, the majority can also be worked over raglan sleeves.

All the garments chosen are classic shapes available everywhere, the knitted fabric heavy enough to carry the weight of the embroidery, and dense enough to prevent the underneath of the stitches showing through to the front.

Any good quality but worn garments in your own wardrobe would provide excellent subjects on which to practise and experiment. Also, this kind of decoration is a wonderful way to disguise damage or wear, and rejuvenate old, but much loved, comfortable clothes.

'Shetland' woollens are readily available in the stores, and have been used for the majority of the woollen garments. But take care to choose one with a fairly close knit if you are planning to embroider a design with small stitches. If the background fabric is too loosely knitted, the smaller stitches may be too heavy for the ground, and they will look uneven. As a general rule, the looser the knitting, the larger the stitch size required.

A perfect ground for most of the woollen knitwear is to be found in the 'fishermen's' knits, Guernseys and Jerseys, but these are rather more expensive to buy.

Fine Botany wool garments should be embroidered only with crewel yarns.

Cotton sweatshirt fabric is a firm, easily embroidered material. For children's wear, which is frequently washed, sweatshirts are ideal. T-shirt fabric is usually a little too thin to carry the more involved designs. Sweatshirts made from a cotton and nylon mix are good to work on: but try to ensure that cotton is the major fibre. Too much nylon gives the fabric a slight sparkle, which is not in keeping with the more traditional designs.

Although the majority of examples in the photographs feature round-necked sweaters and classic cardigans, many of the designs would adapt to other styles. Just remember to keep the basic garment simple.

TOOLS AND EQUIPMENT

To mark guide lines on garments or canvas, use water-soluble pens, which can be bought at any good craft shop. Never use pencil, ballpoint, felt or any other kind of ink pen, as they can run and stain the garment. Tailors' chalk may be used, but avoid dark colours.

Masking tape is used to bind the rough edges of the canvas, not only to avoid it unravelling, but also to prevent it catching or snagging the yarn or woollen fabric as you work. It can be purchased from any good art or craft supplier.

A latch hook is perfect for making up the heavily fringed designs featured in the book. Usually used for rug making, they are available at all good craft shops. A fairly large one is necessary to handle the generous hanks of yarn used to make these particular fringes. If you haven't a latch hook, a crochet hook should be helpful.

You will also need the following general equipment:
- Medium-size scissors (to cut canvas)
- Small sharp (embroidery) scissors
- Stitch ripper
- Tape measure
- Ruler
- Pins
- Tacking threads
- Tweezers (optional)
- Notepad and pencil
- Eraser

STITCHES

CROSS STITCH
(Fig 1)
Used for the majority of designs; easy to do, it completely covers the block of canvas over which it is worked, filling the area with the required square of colour.

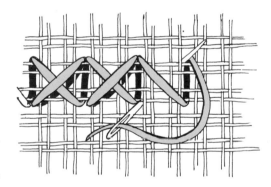

Fig 1:
Cross stitch

To make the embroidery smooth and regular, it is important to ensure that the top diagonal lines (formed by the second half of the stitch) all lie in the same direction. (See illustration.)

Never use a knot to secure this embroidery, as it will eventually pull through the knitted fabric, and also causes a bumpy finish when pressed.

To start, push your needle from the back of the garment to the front of the canvas and draw the thread through both, holding the final 4cm (1½in) at the back, underneath the row that you are about to work; as you embroider, make sure that you trap this tail thread in the back of the stitches.

To finish, pull the thread to the wrong side of the garment and weave 4cm (1½in) through the back of the completed stitches, before cutting off the remainder.

When embroidering blocks of the same colour which are some distance apart, don't carry the yarn in threads longer than 2.5cm (1in): long threads at the back will cause the knitted fabric to lose its stretch, and can also drag some of the embroidered stitches out of shape. Finish as described above, and start again.

BLANKET OR BUTTONHOLE STITCH
(Fig 2)
Can be used as an edging or as a foundation to attach fringing or tassels. Canvas is not needed for this

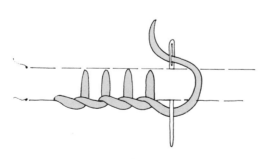

Fig 2:
Blanket or buttonhole stitch

stitch – the size of the stitches is stipulated in the patterns.

For beginners, a tacked or drawn line placed above the stitching line is a helpful guide to measure the height of the upright part of the stitch.

Start buttonhole stitch by making two tight back stitches on the lower line of the stitch. Or, if working along the very edge of the fabric oversew on the edge then weave in the tail of thread later along the back of the row of stitches that you have just made.

CHAIN STITCH
(Fig 3)
Has been used as a convenient elastic stitch to carry a lot of coloured yarns, and as an outline stitch. The size of the stitch is indicated in the patterns.

Fig 3:
Chain stitch

DECORATIVE TRIMMINGS

FRINGES
(Fig 4)
Simple fringes in wool or cotton are attached to a base of buttonhole stitch that has previously been worked onto the garment.

To make the fringing even easier, all the fringes featured are made from cut lengths of the skeins in which the embroidery yarns are packaged. Cutting both ends gives a 15cm (6in) length of yarn, which re-

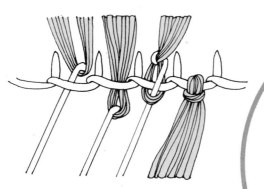

Fig 4:
Fringing over a buttonhole-stitch edge

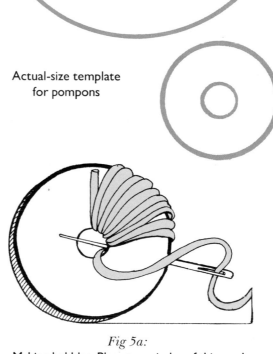

Actual-size template
for pompons

sults in a fringe a little under 7.5cm (3in) long.

First, cut neatly through the loops at both ends of the skein, leaving the paper band in place.

Fringing can be single or multi-coloured. Select the number of lengths stipulated on the pattern, and follow the diagram, spacing each section as instructed. Finally, trim the edge evenly with sharp scissors.

POMPONS OR BOBBLES
(Figs 5a, b and c)
Very small bobbles are often used in rows as decoration. A larger bobble would be used on a hat. The method for making is the same, regardless of size (see diagram).

When a lot of bobbles are required, cut all the pairs of cardboard discs (see template patterns) beforehand, and make them in batches.

The bobbles can be single or multi-coloured. Using a darning or tapestry needle, or bodkin, wrap the yarns tightly over and over, round and round the discs, until you can fit no more through the central hole. When using multi-coloured threads, work about one quarter of the circle at a

Fig 5a:
Making bobbles. Place two circles of thin card together, then wind yarn round and round both until the central hole is completely filled

time, and then change colour. Use the colours randomly and don't cover a colour with itself on a second round of wrapping.

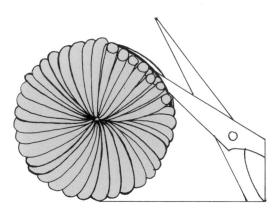

Fig 5b:
Slide point of scissors between the two
circles of card and cut the yarn all round

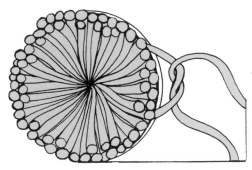

Fig 5c:
Slip a length of yarn or strong thread between
the card circles and tie it tightly round the
yarn at the centre. Then cut away the card,
releasing the yarn, and snip the surface to
form a smoothly rounded ball

Make sure that you use a long piece of thread or yarn to tie the bobble, so that the ends are long enough to thread through a needle to stitch the bobble to the garment.

Finally, snip carefully all over the surface of the bobble to give a smooth, even finish.

TASSELS
(Figs 6a, b, c, d and e)
Large single tassels are used to embellish garments, and are sewn onto the fabric of the garment itself. The tassels can be single or multi-coloured and, like the fringes, are made by cutting through skeins of yarn at one or both ends.

Cutting one end of the skein results in a thread 30cm (12in) long, and will make a tassel almost 15cm (6in) long. Cutting both ends results in a nearly 8cm (3in) tassel. The amount of yarn required for each tassel is stipulated in the individual pattern information.

Leave enough thread through the top loop of the tassel so that it can be threaded through a needle and stitched onto the garment.

Fig 6a:
Making tassels. If using a skein of yarn, cut the
hank at one, or both, ends, leaving the paper
band in place

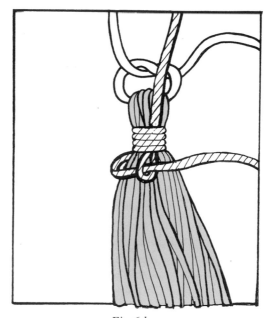

Fig 6b:
Alternatively, wind yarn over a piece of stiff
card the required length of the tassel.
Tie the top loops, leaving long enough ends
to attach the tassel to the garment

Fig 6d:
Whip tightly around the loop to secure it:
then thread the end of the whipping yarn
through the loop and pull, so that the loop
disappears under the whipping

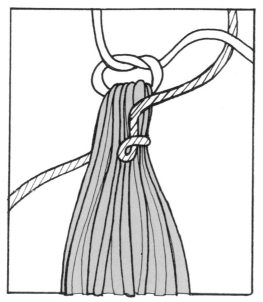

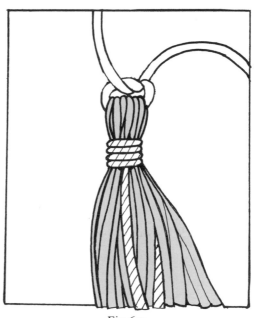

Fig 6c:
Make a loop of self-coloured yarn, leaving
ends as long as the tassel

Fig 6e:
Using a needle, feed the end of the yarn
through the middle of the tassel, and snip the
ends to neaten

CORDS

(Figs 7a, b and c)

Cords appear only once in the book – as a drawstring through a pair of gloves. I was shown the following method of making them in Japan, where it was being used to ply un-spun silk into usable yarn, but it is very useful for many other applications. I have not been able to find another version in any of the standard reference books – although the fortunate Victorian needleworkers were able to buy a little machine with which to make similar cords.

Cord made in this way can be used as a multi-coloured yarn to stitch with, and is also a good method of bulking up crewel yarns to make thicker plies. It is an excellent way to mix different yarns together – wool, cotton, metal threads or silks – to make unusual cords for decoration.

To make (Figs 7a, b and c), twist the yarns around each other by pulling them together down the palms of the hands. Any number of yarns will work, or you could use just two

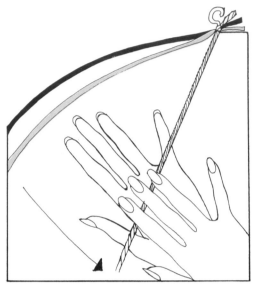

Fig 7b:
Keep the yarn taut to the edge of the palm, then take to the top of the hands and repeat up to twenty times

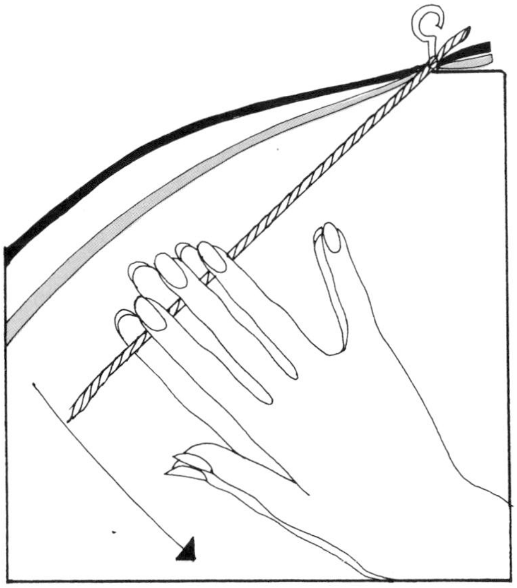

Fig 7a:
Making cords. Take the threads and pull firmly down the palm of the hand, twisting the yarn clockwise

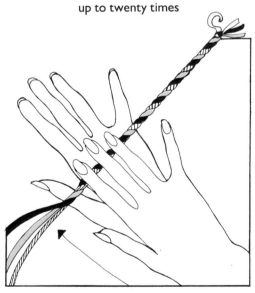

Fig 7c:
When all the threads have been twisted separately, roll them all together anti-clockwise up to fifteen times

colours singly for a simple two-colour braid. The longer the length of yarn, the more twists you will need: as a guideline, one metre (yard) of yarn will require about fifteen twists. The trick is to keep the cords very tight whilst working with them. The Japanese woman who was showing me how to do it taught me to hold the spare cord tight, before and after twisting, by trapping it between my teeth; I still use this method.

BEADING
(Fig 8)

Beads come in many different sizes, and so will need various canvas gauges to accommodate them. The method for working with them is very simple.

For speed and ease, I have used the same colour thread as the background with which to attach the beads. Cotton perle is a strong lustrous thread that comes in a good range of colours: it was used to bead all the items in the book. However, if this is too thick, an extra strong cotton thread could be used.

Although wooden beads usually require a very large gauge of canvas,

Fig 8:
Stitching beads over canvas

they are more suitable than glass for woollen garments, as they are lighter. Knitwear has to be very dense to take the weight of glass beads, which are more suited to sweatshirt fabric.

The basic beading stitch is tent stitch. One line at a time can be worked – changing bead colours as the pattern dictates, or a whole area of one colour can be worked. Make sure all the beads lie in the same direction.

A note of caution: even beads of the same gauge can vary in size and colour from batch to batch, so buy enough to complete the whole project.

PREPARATION

Some designs can be embroidered onto garments without having to undo any seams. However, for your early projects you may find it easier to undo the side seams from the hem to the armhole.

For the designs that have a motif running over the shoulder seams forming a yoke or collar, it is necessary to unpick the underarm and side seams and lay the garment out flat, to enable the waste canvas to be applied and worked on. Carefully unpick the seams using a stitch ripper or small scissors, taking care to cut only the stitches, not the garment. The amount of seam to be unpicked is indicated on every pattern.

When working the designs onto the front or the back of a garment, it is worth cutting a card shape to fit inside (Fig 9). This will prevent you stitching a beautiful piece of embroidery through the front and back

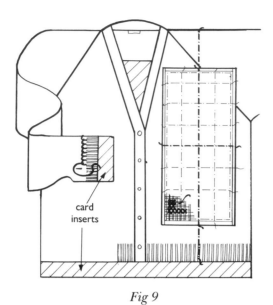

card
inserts

Fig 9

of the work and on to whatever you are wearing!

Cut the piece of card the same size as the width of the garment measured across the chest, and insert it from the hem edge. Do the same for the sleeves, cutting the card to the width of the sleeve at the point where the stitching is to be applied. Insert this card from the shoulder end.

Card inserts are also used when embroidering ribbings that need to retain their elasticity in order to grip the body, like socks, gloves, hats and cuffs. The card stretches the rib to its full extent, so that when the embroidery is finished and the card removed, no elasticity has been lost.

MARKING THE GARMENT
(Fig 10)
In order to ensure that the finished embroidery is correctly positioned, it is essential to have the canvas perfectly aligned on the knitted ground. When embroidering a sweater or sweatshirt, this is easily achieved by

marking and tacking the Centre Front (CF), Centre Back (CB) and, if necessary, the centre of the sleeve (CS). Accuracy is important, because these lines will be matched to the centre of the canvas when it is placed over them. Failure to position the canvas correctly at this stage will result in an off-centre design that *everyone* will notice.

To find and mark these lines:

Lay the garment on an even surface and smooth it out so that it is perfectly flat. Don't stretch it. Measure the width at the shoulder seams, the chest and the hem (above the ribbing), and from the sleeve head (the top of the sleeve at the shoulder seam – or neck, if it is a raglan) to the cuff (above the ribbing). Make a note of these measurements, as you may need them later.

For the CF and CB, divide the body measurements in half and pin the garment at these points. You will find in knitwear that there will be a fairly obvious vertical line of stitches running more or less through the pins; mark this main line by tacking along it with a contrasting coloured thread (avoid dark colours or black, which may leave a mark after they are removed). To avoid tacking the back and front together, insert a piece of card, as previously described.

To find the CS, fold the sleeve along the underarm seam and smooth it flat; then pin along the folded top edge and tack as for the body, following the obvious line of stitches (see Fig 10).

To indicate these points on a sweatshirt, measure and pin as above, holding a ruler between the neck and

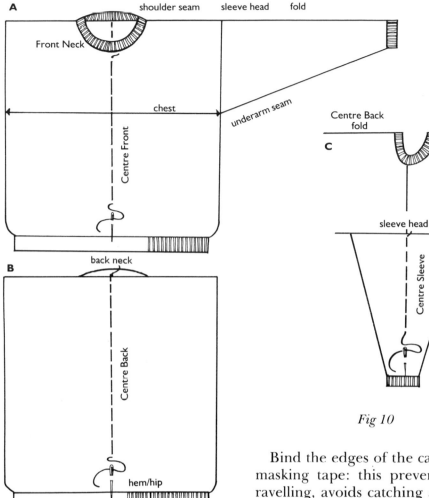

Fig 10

hem points; then tack as already described, or mark with a water-soluble pen or tailors' chalk.

MARKING THE CANVAS
Each charted design indicates the size of canvas required; this is usually 5cm (2in) bigger overall than the actual embroidery, allowing for a 2.5cm (1in) band all round the design. You will also see the positions that need to be marked to correspond with the markings on the garment.

Bind the edges of the canvas with masking tape: this prevents it un-ravelling, avoids catching and snag-ging your embroidery wool, and also protects you and the garment from being scratched.

Find the CF or CB by folding the canvas in half vertically, from top to bottom, and mark the line with a water-soluble pen or tacking stitch. This corresponds with the CF or CB already marked on the garment.

For some of the designs you will need to find the centre point. Fold the canvas in half again, horizontally across the first fold, and mark this line to show the central point where the two lines cross.

APPLYING THE CANVAS TO THE GARMENT
(Fig 11)

Lay the canvas as directed on the garment with the relevant positions aligned, CB on garment to CB of canvas for the back, or CF on garment to CF of canvas for the front. Pin and then securely tack into position. Take care to keep the canvas in the correct position while you do this. In the case of a large piece of canvas, a grid of tacking stitches should be worked over the entire surface, forming approximately 8cm (3in) squares, to ensure that no slipping occurs. Indications of where this is necessary are given on the placing diagrams for each design.

When tacking these lines, make sure that no stretching of the underneath garment occurs. It is advisable to turn the garment to the wrong side after securing the centres and outside edges. You will find it easier to keep the knitted fabric absolutely smooth

and flat if you tack from this side.

When placing canvas close to the rib, you may find that this part of the garment keeps springing back, and won't fit. Don't worry; as long as you have checked that the overall area of embroidery will fit within the width of the chest measurement (from under arm to under arm) it will be all right. Just coax the canvas into position, pinning it evenly as you go – though the rib may tend to curl over the canvas when fully stretched.

You are now ready to begin the embroidery. The exact starting point is specified on each chart and in each set of instructions.

FINISHING

When the work is complete, cut away some of the surplus canvas, leaving sufficient around the embroidery to allow enough thread to get a grip on, so that you can pull it out.

Dampen the canvas threads until they become limp, using either a plant spray, or placing a damp cloth over the work and pressing lightly.

On a large piece of work you may have to dampen the canvas several times, and wet it very thoroughly on a densely stitched section.

Start to pull the threads out from under the embroidery *one by one* (Fig 12), from the outside, working in. Use tweezers if necessary. When all the threads are removed, loosely shake the garment to enable the embroidery to settle.

The whole area of embroidery now needs to be *lightly* steam-pressed. This is to even out the texture of the

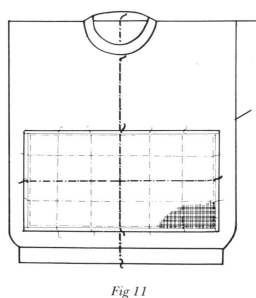

Fig 11

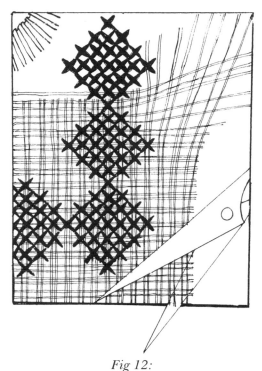

Fig 12:
Cutting away the outer surplus canvas, prior to dampening it and pulling out the threads, one by one

stitches; avoid heavy pressing, which will flatten the surface.

It is always advisable to press embroidery from the back, so turn the garment inside out and place it on a padded surface, to prevent the stitches from becoming flattened. Put a layer of fabric, ideally a clean towel, inside or underneath the garment. Gently pat the embroidery into the correct position and check the measurements with those that you took prior to starting the embroidery, to ensure that there is no distortion.

Taking care not to stretch the fabric, place a clean, damp cloth over the whole area of the embroidery and press with a warm iron, or a steam setting over a dry cloth. Press with an up and down motion of the iron:

don't rub backwards and forwards, as if taking out creases. If the garment has shrunk or stretched, pin it out flat to its original size and press with a damp cloth, avoiding the pins, and leave to dry still pinned out.

If the knitting has been stretched when placing the canvas, the embroidered design may not look evenly balanced. There is no need to panic if this occurs. Keeping the garment flat, coax the embroidery into the correct position – measuring each side so that it is level, and stretching or pushing the knitting together slightly. When it is aligned, pin it into position to the ironing board or towel. Steam and press as before. If necessary, repeat this several times until the fault is corrected.

When the garment is dry and cool, unpin and lightly shake it. If the seams have been unpicked, sew it back together either by hand using a back stitch, or by machine using a zig-zag stretch stitch. Lightly press the finished seam with a damp cloth or steam iron.

Turn to the right side. Then rush to a mirror and try it on.

LAUNDERING

Your inexpensive garment is now a precious item, and needs to be treated as such.

Although dry cleaning is recommended for tapestry wool embroidery, I prefer to wash knitted garments by hand, using a special cold water washing liquid. Gently squeeze out the excess water, then lay the garment out flat in the correct shape (preferably on a clean towel), and leave it to dry away from direct heat.

Sweatshirts embroidered with cottons can be washed by machine. Turn the garment inside out and use cool settings for water and drying temperatures.

You may find that the wet canvas leaves a residue of stiffening size that marks the sweatshirts. This disappears with a cool wash.

ADAPTING DESIGNS

The size of each design, as it is photographed and charted, is shown in the individual instructions.

If you wish, for example, to use an adult's chart to embroider a sweatshirt for a child, you will need to change the scale of the design. To do this, you must calculate the area the design will cover when it is worked over different gauges of canvas. When you have done this, you will be able to decide how much the design should be reduced to fit the smaller garment. And thus, the gauge of canvas to buy.

The following tables will enable you to estimate the measurements of a design, worked on any gauge of canvas, over one set of threads or two.

1 Count the number of squares on the chart that you wish to adapt, widthways and lengthways. One square = one stitch.
2 Note the measurements of the original (adult) design, and the number of stitches per 2.5cm (1in).
3 Estimate the gauge of canvas that *might* give you a suitable reduction (remembering that the more

stitches to 2.5cm/1in, the smaller the design).
4 Find the table for the gauge of canvas that you are considering, and work out the measurements, based on the number of stitches in the design (step 1 above).

For instance, supposing the design is 20 stitches deep x 175 stitches wide (step 1), and the adult version is worked over *five* stitches to 2.5cm (1in) (step 2), resulting in an overall measurement of 87.5cm (35in) x 10cm (4in).

To calculate the size that the design would be when worked over a canvas with *eight* stitches to 2.5cm (1in) (step 3), use the appropriate table below A(i). This will give you:

Depth: 20 stitches = 6.25cm (2½in)
Width: 175 stitches (100+50+20+5) = 54.5cm (21½in)

If this measurement fits happily on your sweatshirt, this gauge of canvas (8 holes/stitches to 2.5cm/1in) is the one to buy. But if it is still a little too large, calculate the measurements if the design was worked over 10 holes to 2.5cm (1in), using table B(i).

Designs can, of course, be enlarged in exactly the same way.

If you reduce a design by a large amount, you will find it necessary to use a finer yarn than that stipulated in the instructions for the original garment. Turn to page 8 (Yarns) for guidance, and then experiment to find the most suitable. Tapestry wool works well with an 8 holes per 2.5cm (1in) canvas, and larger stitches, but crewel wools are more suitable for 10,

TABLE A: CANVAS WITH EIGHT HOLES per 2.5cm (1in)

(i) Working 8 stitches to 2.5cm (1in):	5 stitches = 1.5cm ($\frac{5}{8}$in)
	10 stitches = 3cm (1$\frac{1}{4}$in)
	20 stitches = 6.25cm (2$\frac{1}{2}$in)
	30 stitches = 9.5cm (3$\frac{3}{4}$in)
	40 stitches = 12.5cm (5in)
	50 stitches = 15.5cm (6$\frac{1}{8}$in)
	100 stitches = 31.25cm (12$\frac{1}{4}$in)
(ii) Working (over two threads) 4 stitches to 2.5cm (1in):	5 stitches = 3cm (1$\frac{1}{4}$in)
	10 stitches = 6.25cm (2$\frac{1}{2}$in)
	20 stitches = 12.5cm (5in)
	30 stitches = 18.75cm (7$\frac{3}{8}$in)
	40 stitches = 25cm (10in)
	50 stitches = 31.25 (12$\frac{1}{4}$in)
	100 stitches = 62.5cm (25in)

TABLE B: CANVAS WITH TEN HOLES per 2.5cm (1in)

(i) Working 10 stitches to 2.5cm (1in):	5 stitches = 1.25cm ($\frac{1}{2}$in)
	10 stitches = 2.5cm (1in)
	20 stitches = 5cm (2in)
	30 stitches = 7.5cm (3in)
	40 stitches = 10cm (4in)
	50 stitches = 12.5cm (5in)
	100 stitches = 25cm (10in)
(ii) Working (over two threads) 5 stitches to 2.5cm (1in):	5 stitches = 2.5cm (1in)
	10 stitches = 5cm (2in)
	20 stitches = 10cm (4in)
	30 stitches = 15cm (6in)
	40 stitches = 20cm (8in)
	50 stitches = 25cm (10in)
	100 stitches = 50cm (20in)

12 and 14 holes per 2.5cm (1in) canvas. Stranded cottons (floss) present no problem, as they can be divided or added to.

It is always wise to work a sample section first, just to be safe. A 2.5cm (1in) square of solid stitching will give you a clear indication of how easily the yarn will pull through the canvas, and how the finished work will look.

TABLE C: CANVAS WITH TWELVE HOLES per 2.5cm (1in)

(i) Working 12 stitches to 2.5cm (1in):	5 stitches = 1cm ($\frac{3}{8}$in)
	10 stitches = 2cm ($\frac{3}{4}$in)
	20 stitches = 4cm (1$\frac{1}{2}$in)
	30 stitches = 6cm (2$\frac{3}{8}$in)
	40 stitches = 8.25cm (3$\frac{1}{4}$in)
	50 stitches = 10.5cm (4$\frac{1}{8}$in)
	100 stitches = 21cm (8$\frac{1}{4}$in)
(ii) Working (over two threads) 6 stitches to 2.5cm (1in):	5 stitches = 2cm ($\frac{3}{4}$in)
	10 stitches = 4cm (1$\frac{1}{2}$in)
	20 stitches = 8.25cm (3$\frac{1}{4}$in)
	30 stitches = 12.5cm (5in)
	40 stitches = 16.5cm (6$\frac{1}{2}$in)
	50 stitches = 21cm (8$\frac{1}{4}$in)
	100 stitches = 41.5cm (16$\frac{1}{2}$in)

TABLE D: CANVAS WITH FOURTEEN HOLES per 2.5cm (1in)

(i) Working 14 stitches to 2.5cm (1in):	5 stitches = 1cm ($\frac{3}{8}$in)
	10 stitches = 1.75cm ($\frac{5}{8}$in)
	20 stitches = 3.5cm (1$\frac{3}{8}$in)
	30 stitches = 5.25cm (2$\frac{1}{8}$in)
	40 stitches = 7cm (2$\frac{3}{4}$in)
	50 stitches = 9cm (3$\frac{1}{2}$in)
	100 stitches = 17.75cm (7in)
(ii) Working (over two threads) 7 stitches to 2.5cm (1in):	5 stitches = 1.75cm ($\frac{5}{8}$in)
	10 stitches = 3.5cm (1$\frac{3}{8}$in)
	20 stitches = 7cm (2$\frac{3}{4}$in)
	30 stitches = 10.75cm (4$\frac{1}{4}$in)
	40 stitches = 14.25cm (5$\frac{5}{8}$in)
	50 stitches = 17.75cm (7in)
	100 stitches = 35.75cm (14in)

DESIGN NOTES

Looking through the designs, you will see that the majority are composed from a number of separate motifs. These can, of course, be used in many different ways: either re-arranged within the same design – or individual motifs from two or more designs combined to create something new and completely original. The range of motifs offers endless opportunities to create an immense number of exciting designs of your own.

If you plan to do this, try to stay within one group of work; for example, choose a range of items from the sampler section, or combine pieces from Berlin woolwork. This will give your design a sense of co-ordination and authenticity. But you can take your choice from the decorative trimmings, all of which will go with everything.

The best way to work out your own design is to re-chart the original design or motifs onto graph papers that are the same size as the canvas that you wish to embroider. You will find sample graph papers at the end of the book. This will give you an immediate impression of how your design will look, and what size it will appear when worked.

When deciding what size to embroider a design, you will find that drawing it to scale on graph tracing paper is invaluable, as you can then place the design tracing on top of the garment and assess how well it fits. This eliminates any danger of looking at your finished embroidery and wondering whether the design might have been more effective had it been larger or smaller.

The special tracing paper, called Hobby Graph Paper, is graphed to the same sizes as the canvases used in embroidery. The sizes are: 8, 10, 12, 14, 16 and 20 squares per 2.5cm (1in). When calculating 7, 6, 5 and 4 stitches per 2.5cm (1in), simply double up the charted squares as you do when working the embroidery. Any good stationers should supply this paper.

BACK DESIGNS

As a designer, I dislike blank backs on garments, particularly on those that are hand-embroidered. Although few back views are shown in the photographs, most of the designs have at least a small motif on the back, echoing the main motif on the front. Sometimes a band on the front hem is repeated around the back hem, and occasionally the entire design is repeated.

The planning of these back designs is to be found on the placing charts, and all design quantities for canvas and yarn include the back designs. Any other information is included for each individual design.

SIDE SEAMS

To enable the designs to fit different sizes of garment, none of them, although they may appear continuous, actually extend to the back. There is a small gap, and then the band is repeated on the back. Care must be taken to align these corresponding front and back bands at the side seam.

BUTTONS

Often the buttons on cardigans look out of place after the garment has been embroidered. Either find new colours to match or tone with the design, as illustrated – or cover your own with yarn, using a commercial kit available at craft shops and large stores.

DECORATIVE
EFFECTS

◆

In this first section you will find a range of embroideries that even a beginner can tackle with confidence. They use the familiar embroidery stitches – chain, buttonhole or blanket, and cross stitch – and introduce the stitches, trimmings and techniques used throughout the book. Progressing from basic trims to using small pieces of canvas for charted designs, they give a foretaste of what is to come!

There are lots of easy ideas that children might enjoy making. Not just sweaters and sweatshirts, but hats, gloves, scarves and socks have been embroidered, tasselled, bobbled, fringed and even beaded.

In case you would welcome some guidance when choosing colour schemes, I have put together four Anchor colour ranges to choose from: DARK, BRIGHT, PASTEL and SUBTLE (see photograph illustrating colour swatches in wool and cotton). Each range has six colours in it: red, orange, yellow, green, blue and violet – almost a rainbow. Because the colour ranges are my own personal choice, they reflect my own preferences. For instance, I love 'shocking pink', and prefer it to red: so my Bright range starts with pink.

Any garment in this section of the book can be stitched in any of the four colour ranges: the choice depends on your own preference and the background colour that you are working on.

However, these ranges are only suggestions. If you have ideas or strong tastes of your own, ignore them and plan your own colourways. For instance, the Bright range doesn't include the brightest colours available, which are often garish, and should be avoided except for wearing in very bright conditions, such as the beach or on the ski-slopes. On the other hand, many of these designs would look stunning embroidered in just one or two contrasting colours.

It is sensible to take your garment along to the shop when you buy your yarns. Select the individual colours from the range of your choice and place them against the garment to be embroidered. This will help you to assess the overall effect.

Throughout the book, most of the chosen garments are in muted colours, and in styles that are generally available. Black, navy, bottle green, grey, beige, cream and white all provide good backgrounds which complement most of the colour ranges. However, there are some brightly coloured ones too, embroidered with a selection of hot, zingy colours from the Bright range.

The Pastel range is easy to work with, looking good on very dark or subtle grounds, as well as the obvious creams and white.

The Bright range can be used on practically any coloured ground except very soft shades, which will fade in comparison to the strong colours.

The Subtle and Dark ranges need more care – although they are usually the easiest to wear. These ranges are subdued, and need neutral or very dark grounds. Against brightly coloured grounds they will look dirty and drab.

If you find that your background colour is one of the six colours in the range, look at the whole range of yarns and choose another version of that colour with a similar tone. The tapestry wool and stranded cotton (floss) ranges are so wide that it is usually possible to find another complementary colour. Select an alternative colour and place it amongst your chosen colour range, half-closing your eyes to see if the overall effect is harmonious. If you don't feel it blends in well, try another shade: trial and error at this stage is the only way to get it right.

Most of the following designs use tapestry wools, as they make the plumpest bobbles, tassels and fringes with which to decorate woollen garments. For cotton garments, 'soft cotton' is good for making tassels and fringes, and 'stranded cotton' (floss) best for cross-stitch embroidery, as you can separate the strands for finer work. The ranges are given in colours available in both stranded and soft cotton (floss).

Should you want to adapt any of these ideas in wool for babies and toddlers, use crewel wools, as they have a finer ply and will look less bulky. Stranded cottons (floss) can be worked successfully on cotton garments, using less than the six strands for finer effects.

If you decide to make the beaded garments, choose the beads first, the yarns second and the garment third. Colours of beads are variable, but a very soft muted collection of the Subtle colour range is often the most effective.

WOOL

RED	ORANGE	YELLOW	GREEN	BLUE	PURPLE
8490	9028	8140	8969	8610	8594

BRIGHT

| 88 | 925 | 303 | 187 | 132 | 111 |

COTTON

WOOL

RED	ORANGE	YELLOW	GREEN	BLUE	PURPLE
8426	9602	8046	9028	8740	8596

DARK

| 897 | 352 | 310 | 683 | 150 | 112 |

COTTON

Colour swatches showing the BRIGHT
(upper two rows) and DARK (lower two
rows) ranges of Anchor embroidery wools (above)
and cottons (below)

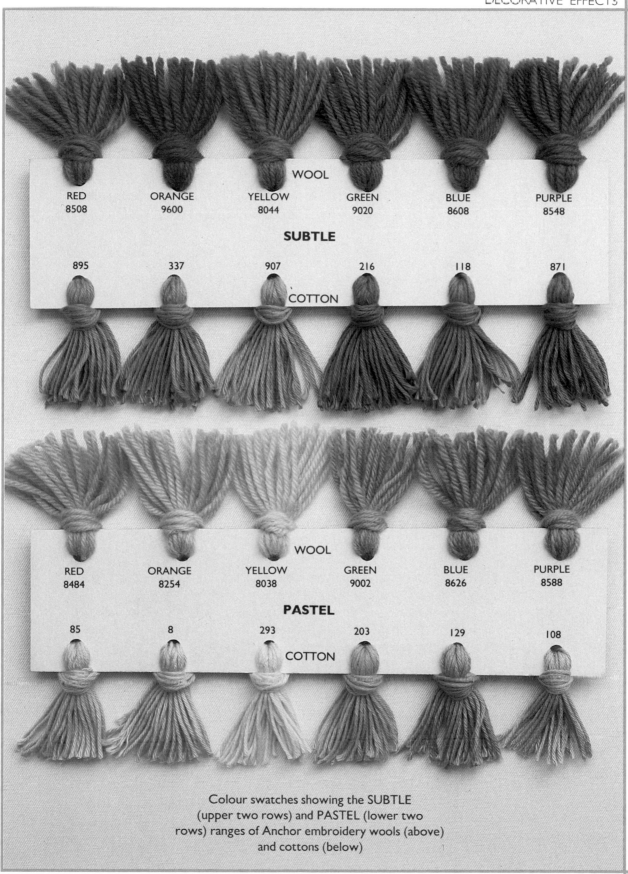

WOOL

RED	ORANGE	YELLOW	GREEN	BLUE	PURPLE
8508	9600	8044	9020	8608	8548

SUBTLE

| 895 | 337 | 907 | 216 | 118 | 871 |

COTTON

WOOL

RED	ORANGE	YELLOW	GREEN	BLUE	PURPLE
8484	8254	8038	9002	8626	8588

PASTEL

| 85 | 8 | 293 | 203 | 129 | 108 |

COTTON

Colour swatches showing the SUBTLE
(upper two rows) and PASTEL (lower two
rows) ranges of Anchor embroidery wools (above)
and cottons (below)

◄ Woman's cardigan chain stitched in separate colours of the Subtle range, and a child's sweater in blended colours from the Bright range. All finished off with individual tassels

MULTI-COLOURED CHAIN-STITCH SWEATERS

Chain stitch is a wonderful way to transform a garment with instant colour and texture. It makes a neat fine line when stitched with one thread, and has been used for centuries as a strong outlining stitch and it can also be used to create intricate patterns. The two garments in the photograph demonstrate just how simple and effective the colour ranges can be. By threading six colours at once through a needle or bodkin, and working giant stitches, the colours blend in a fascinating and subtle way. If you want a stronger impact, try using one colour at a time, in sequence.

Follow alongside the seams of a basic sweater (don't attempt to sew through the actual seam – it's too thick): or work a simple criss-cross pattern across the front and back. It's both surprising and encouraging to discover how little experience is required to achieve such impressive results.

Note: Sweatshirt fabric is too dense to take this design, but it could be worked in cotton onto a cotton knitted sweater.

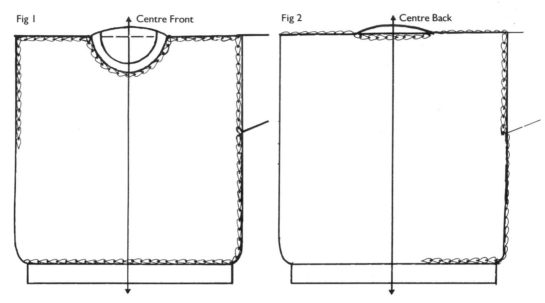

Fig I   Centre Front   Fig 2   Centre Back

GARMENT

Loosely knitted woollen garment with raglan or set-in, T-shaped sleeves

YARN

Anchor Tapestry Wool (Yarn)

NUMBER OF SKEINS

Dark Range:

8426 x 3 Red	9028 x 3 Green	
9602 x 3 Orange	8740 x 3 Blue	
8046 x 3 Yellow	8596 x 3 Violet	

I Measure and note down the lengths of all the seams to be chain stitched as shown on Figs 1 and 2.

2 Use lengths of approximately 1 metre (1yd) of yarn at a time. You will need to make several threadings to complete each length of stitching.

3 It is important to keep the stitches around the neck, wrist and bottom edges fairly loose, so that they don't restrict the elasticity of the garment. Make card inserts (Basic Instructions) when stitching around the ribs, to prevent this happening.

4 Using a darning needle and working on the wrong side (WS), take one colour at a time (any order) and make back stitches in the seam allowance at the top of one side seam, to secure each thread.

5 When all the yarns are secure, thread them together in a bodkin or large darning needle and take them through to the right side (RS). Always push your needle *between* the knitted threads: it is hard to pull the needle through split threads.

6 Using all six colours at once, work along one side of a seam, making each stitch approximately 2cm (¾in) long. The stitches should be close enough to the seam to overlap it.

7 To finish take the yarns through to the wrong side and weave each one individually through the back of the stitches for approximately 5cm (2in).

8 Remeasure all the stitched lines and check against the original measurements taken at the start. If necessary, stretch and steam as described in the Basic Instructions.

FRINGED SWEATSHIRT
WITH GLOVES, SOCKS AND TASSELLED HAT

Multi-coloured cotton yarns are attached to a base of buttonhole stitch to enliven sweatshirts, socks and gloves; a single tassel makes a colourful hat trim. Buttonhole is a useful stitch, as the structure allows for some 'give' on knitwear, and it is possible to work it on the main body as well as the edges of garments.

When working along the ribs on socks and gloves, insert pieces of card so that they are fully stretched (see Basic Instructions). They will revert to the correct size when released.

GARMENT
Child's sweatshirt with T-shape, set-in or raglan sleeves

YARNS
Anchor Soft Embroidery Cotton

NUMBER OF SKEINS
Bright Range:
88 x 2   Red
925 x 2   Orange
303 x 2   Yellow
187 x 2   Green
132 x 2   Blue
111 x 2   Violet
Background colour x 1

1 Take a 5cm (2in) measurement all round the neck, from the lower edge of the rib, so that it radiates out in a circle. Mark every 1cm (½in) with a water-soluble pen. Join up all these measured points to make a continuous line (Fig 1). (Increase this measurement for a larger garment: up to 10cm/4in if necessary.) 5mm (¼in) above this line, draw in another line as a guide for the height of the buttonhole stitches (Fig 1).
2 Using a crewel needle, work a row of buttonhole stitches using one thread of a yarn to match the garment. Make the stitches 5mm (¼in) apart, with the vertical threads pointing towards the neck.

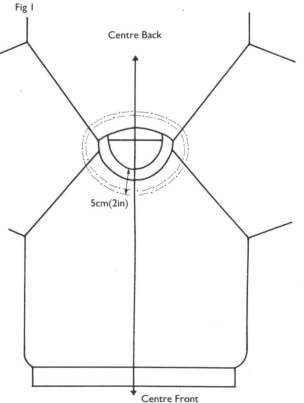

Fig I

Centre Back

5cm(2in)

Centre Front

◄ A brightly coloured cotton fringe makes a lively contrast trim for sweatshirt and socks with woollen tassels for gloves. A single tassel makes a colourful hat trim

◄ Simple multi-coloured pastel fringes in cotton on a child's polo shirt. Change the buttons to match the fringes

3   To make the fringe, cut each skein through at either end, keeping the paper bands in place. (see Basic Instructions).

4   Draw out one thread in each of the following colours: Yellow/Blue/Pink.

   Make a fringe through the bottom edge of the buttonhole stitch, using all three colours together.

5   Repeat on next stitch using Orange/Green/Purple.

6   Continue to alternate these colour blends, using three threads per fringe. You may find a latch hook or crochet hook helpful.

7   When complete, trim the edge of the fringe in a straight line with sharp scissors.

GLOVES, SOCKS AND TASSELLED HAT

1   To buttonhole ribbed edges, stretch the ribs to their widest measurement, as in Fig 2.

2   Cut a piece of card to this width x 5cm (2in) deep.

3   Place the card in position so that the ribbing remains fully stretched whilst stitching (Fig 2).

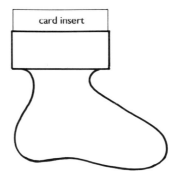

card insert

4   Work buttonhole stitch along the outer edge of the rib.

5   Remove the card.

6   Make the fringes as you did for the sweatshirt.

For the hat: See tassel making in the Basic Instructions. Use ten threads of each colour, having cut the skeins at one end only to make 30cm (12in) lengths of yarn.

CHAIN STITCH AND BOBBLE CARDIGAN
WITH HAT, GLOVES AND SCARF

Most people had fun making pompons and bobbles as children. I have used them on this typical school cardigan to turn it into a smart and colourful jacket. Multi-coloured buttons complement the embroidery. Very young children would enjoy wearing the amusing hat, gloves and scarf.

Careful measuring is the secret to ensure the tramlines are always exactly parallel and neatly chain stitched. The twisted braid used here as a drawstring for the gloves has many uses. In fine yarns it would make an interesting embroidery thread for loosely knitted woollen garments.

GARMENTS
V-neck or round-neck woollen cardigan
Knitted hat and gloves
Knitted or wool fabric scarf

YARN
Anchor Tapestry Wool

NUMBER OF SKEINS
Bright Range:

8969 x 5	Green	9028 x 5	Orange
8610 x 5	Blue	8594 x 5	Purple
8490 x 5	Pink	8140 x 5	Yellow

1 Fasten the cardigan and lay it out flat (Fig 1). Measure the front across the chest from underarm to underarm.

2 Cut a piece of card to this size x 12cm (5in) deep and insert across the bottom of the buttoned-up cardigan (Fig 1).

◄ Rows of brightly coloured chains and bobbles transform a school cardigan and plain hat. The gloves and hat have matching drawstrings and bobbles

3 Measure around the sleeve 5cm (2in) above the top of the ribbing.

4 Cut a piece of card to half this size x 8cm (3in) deep. Place it inside the sleeve rib (Fig 1).

5 Pin and tack, or mark with a water-soluble pen, the lines drawn on Figs 1 and 2, measuring them exactly 2.5cm (1in) apart.

6 Measure approximately 45cm (18in) lengths of each of the six colours to be used.

7 Start chain stitching at dot on Line 1 (Fig 1) at right-hand side seam, making the loops about 12-13mm (½in) in length. Start with the Blue yarn and continue in this colour sequence: Blue/Pink/Green/Yellow/Purple/Orange/Blue . . .

8 Stitch all round line 1 to meet at the side seam.

9 Repeat for line 3, starting at the point marked on Fig 1, beginning with a different colour.

10 Cut shorter lengths of each yarn to stitch lines 4 and 6 on the sleeves.

11 You will need to sew on a bobble approximately every 5cm (2in). (See

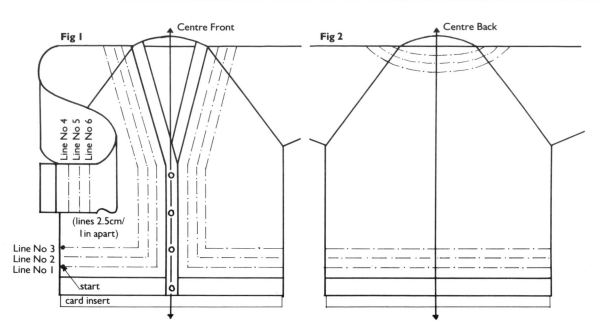

Fig 1 · Centre Front

Line No 4
Line No 5
Line No 6

(lines 2.5cm/ 1 in apart)

Line No 3
Line No 2
Line No 1

start

card insert

Fig 2 · Centre Back

Basic Instructions, Pompons or Bobbles.) To calculate the number of bobbles that you will have to make, measure the whole length of line 2.

For example: length of line 2:
173cm (69in)
Number of bobbles:
$173 \div 5 \ (69 \div 2) = 34$

12 Divide this amount by six, then make up the appropriate number in each of the six colours: eg $34 \div 6 = 5$ (remainder 4) = 5 bobbles of each colour. Make up the remaining four in one of each of the colours from the sequence, starting with Blue.

13 For each sleeve, make one bobble of each colour.

14 Measure along line 2 from point A to CB and mark every 5cm (2in).

15 Measure from point B to CB and mark every 5cm (2in).

Any discrepancy in the 5cm (2in) intervals can be adjusted at the back of the neck: the way the bobbles fall when applied will hide this adjustment.

16 Measure from point B and around the back to point A, and mark every 5cm (2in), making any adjustments at the side seams.

17 Sew a Blue bobble at point A and continue up the front of the cardigan across the back neck and down to point B, using the same colour sequence. *Note*: The colours will not match on either side of the cardigan (see photograph).

18 Continue from point B in colour sequence around the back to the side seam.

19 From point A sew bobbles to this same side seam working *backwards* through the colour sequence. As it is unlikely that you will get an even distribution of colours, this ensures that any discrepancy in the sequence is tucked away under the arm at the side seam.

20 On the sleeves, stitch one bobble on line 5 at the CS point and then one 5cm (2in) away on either side. Use bobbles in the first three colours of the sequence on one sleeve, and the other colours on the second sleeve.

Bobbles and chain stitches alternate to form yokes, and a scarf with bobbles attached to buttonhole edging, show off the Dark, Subtle and Pastel colour ranges

HAT, GLOVES AND SCARF

1 Measure the wearer's head and cut a 10cm (4in) deep piece of card to half this measurement. Fit inside the hat to stretch the ribbing, so that it will retain its elasticity.

2 Chain stitch two lines around the rib of the hat, using the yarns in the same colour sequence as on the cardigan.

3 Stitch on bobbles at approximately 5cm (2in) intervals in between the two lines of chain stitching, still keeping to the original colour sequence.

4 Cut a piece of card to stretch the cuffs of the gloves, and fit inside the ribbing.

5 Make up a cord for each glove (see Basic Instructions), by twisting together 140cm (1½yd) lengths of each of the six colours. Initially twist the Yellow, Pink and Blue together, and then the Orange, Green and Purple: finally roll these two blends together to make one cord.

6 Thread the cord through a bodkin or large darning needle and work in small running stitches around the glove, just on the inside edge of the cuff.

7 Attach one bobble to each end of the cord, and then tie it in a bow.

8 Using a matching yarn, work buttonhole stitch around all the edges of the scarf (see Basic Instructions).

9 Fringe through this stitch every 5cm (2in) (see Basic Instructions), working in the same colour sequence as that for the stitching and bobbles on the cardigan and hat.

BOBBLE AND FRINGE CARDIGAN

I have worked this cardigan in the Dark colourway to demonstrate how different colour schemes completely change the effect of the same trimmings. Here the bobbles look sumptuous, and not so frivolous as the child's Bright version, the depth of colour being increased by the cut ends of the yarn. The encrusted yoke has great style, and could be worn with any classic winter clothes – imagine it with velvets and corduroys, or echoing rich tartans.

Alternatively, make it in the Bright colourway on a dark ground for a glowing, jewel-like yoked jacket to brighten up dull winter days.

This extravagantly decorative design is a little more involved than the previous garments, so wait until you have some experience of the technique before you attempt this one.

GARMENT
Button-through round-neck
cardigan, medium-gauge knit

YARN
Anchor Tapestry Wool

NUMBER OF SKEINS
Dark Range:
9602 x 6   Rust
8740 x 6   Blue
8426 x 7   Burgundy
8596 x 7   Purple
9028 x 7   Green
8046 x 7   Ochre

TO BUTTONHOLE
Use self-coloured 4-ply yarn

◄ A combination of bobbles and fringe in
the Dark colour range creates a richly
textured yoke on a plain cardigan

1 For the front of the cardigan, button it up and lay it out flat (Fig 1) (overleaf).
2 Measure across the cardigan from CF to sleeve seams, and mark the halfway point.
3 Tack in a vertical line at this point from shoulder seam to rib (line 1).
4 Measure along the shoulder seam from the neck rib to line 1.
5 Measure this same distance down the button band from the neck rib, and mark in a horizontal line (line 2) from this point to line 1.
6 This forms the inner yoke.
7 Mark or tack another line 5mm (¼in) within this yoke (line 3), to act as a guide for the buttonhole stitching.
8 Measure the distance along the shoulder seam from the sleeve seam to line 1.
9 Measure this same distance down the button band from line 1, and mark or tack a horizontal line across to meet the sleeve seam (line 4).
10 This forms the outer yoke.
11 Mark/tack a line 5mm (¼in)

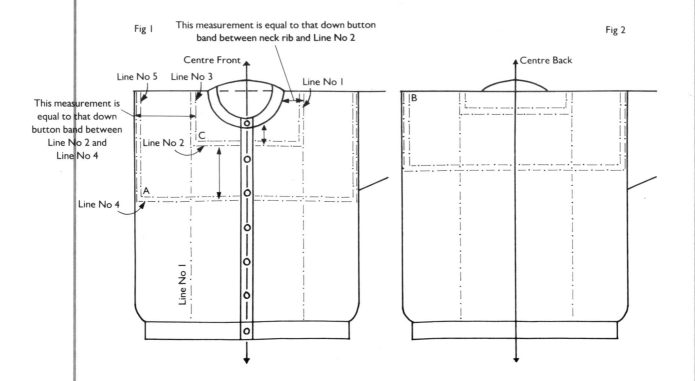

Fig 1

This measurement is equal to that down button band between neck rib and Line No 2

Fig 2

Centre Front

Centre Back

Line No 5   Line No 3

Line No 1

This measurement is equal to that down button band between Line No 2 and Line No 4

Line No 2

C

A

Line No 4

Line No 1

B

within this yoke as a guide for the buttonhole stitch (line 5).

12 For the back of the cardigan (Fig 2), mark in CB from neck to hem (see Basic Instructions).

13 Repeat the same procedure as you followed for the front of the cardigan. (*Note*: the back yoke is not so deep – because the neckline is higher.)

14 Buttonhole stitch around all the marked lines, with the continuous edge of the stitch on the outer line, and the vertical threads pointing towards the neck.

15 Make up six bobbles in each of the six colours (see Basic Instructions).

16 Starting at point A marked on Fig 1, sew on a Blue bobble. Then, working in the sequence Blue/ Burgundy / Green / Ochre / Purple /

Rust/Blue, sew bobbles across the front, spacing them evenly, approximately every 5cm (2in), to the opposite corner. Then, with the same spacing, sew bobbles up the yoke to the shoulder seam (see photograph).

17 Returning to the first Blue bobble, but working the colour sequence *backwards*, sew bobbles up this side of the yoke to the shoulder seam – Blue/Rust/Purple/Ochre/ Green/Burgundy (see photograph).

18 Turning the cardigan over to work the back, start at point B marked on Fig 2, and continue to sew on bobbles, following on the colour sequence from the front.

19 Position one bobble (any colour) at point C marked on Fig 1 within the inner yoke, and then sew one up from this and one across (following the colour sequence), spacing the

Bobbles and fringes
make yokes of single
and blended colours,
in the Pastel and
Subtle ranges

bobbles the same distance apart as on
the outer yoke.

20 Repeat, using the three remaining colours on the other side – same spacing as the outer yoke (see photograph).

21 On the back, sew a row of bobbles in the colour sequence, spacing them evenly within the inner yoke.

22 Apply tassels (see Basic Instructions) to the buttonhole stitch, working in the same colour sequence, but starting at any point with any of the six colours. Place the tassels so that they fall between each bobble, as illustrated.

CHILD'S TRIANGLE AND TASSEL SWEATER

This cross stitch design is an introduction to using canvas to stitch basic shapes. The yoke goes across the shoulders and onto the back. An even simpler version that doesn't entail opening up the side and underarm sleeve seams has been illustrated. If you like, you can use the front section of the chart by itself and build up rows of triangles to create geometric effects that rely on stripes of colour.

The Pastel shades look fresh and pretty for a child's cotton sweater, but the design would work just as well using wools in the stronger colours.

GARMENT
Child's knitted or cotton round-necked sweater with set-in T-shape sleeve

YARNS
Either Anchor Stranded Cotton (floss) or Anchor Soft Embroidery Cotton

NUMBER OF SKEINS
Pastel Range:

85 x 3	Pink
108 x 2	Mauve
203 x 2	Green
8 x 3	Peach
293 x 3	Yellow
129 x 3	Blue

CANVAS GAUGE
8 holes per 2.5cm (1in)

QUANTITY
48 x 38cm (19 x 15in)

◄ Cottons from the Pastel range make a fresh and pretty yoke for a child's jumper — and her doll has a matching T-shirt. The cross stitch embroidery is worked over canvas

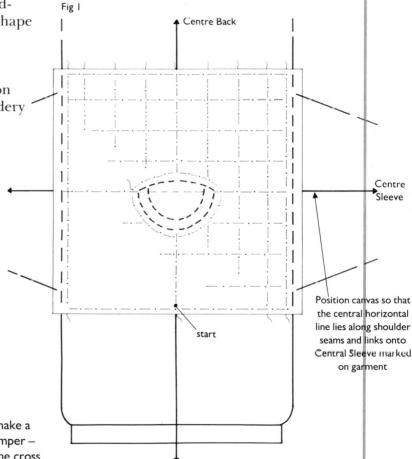

Fig 1

Centre Back

Centre Sleeve

start

Centre Front

Position canvas so that the central horizontal line lies along shoulder seams and links onto Central Sleeve marked on garment

STITCH SIZE
4 stitches to 2.5cm (1in)
(Embroider over every other hole)

EMBROIDERED AREA
43 x 33cm (17 x 13in)

TASSELS
Approximately 7cm (2¾in) long

1 Open the side and sleeve seams of the garment from the hem through to the cuffs (Fig 1) see page 45.
2 Lay the garment out flat and mark CF and CB and down the CS.
3 Prepare and mark the canvas as explained in the Basic Instructions.
4 Fold the canvas in half horizontally and mark the centre line.

5 Position the canvas as shown in Fig 1: pin and tack it into place, making a grid of stitches to secure it firmly, and prevent it slipping.
6 On the wrong side, tack the canvas and garment around the inner edge of the neck, taking care to keep it even.
7 Using two threads of yarn, start to embroider the cross stitch (see Basic Instructions) at the point marked on the chart, working over every other hole of the canvas.
8 Remove the canvas (see Basic Instructions).

▼ Chart to make the triangle and tassel yoke for a child's sweater in the Pastel range

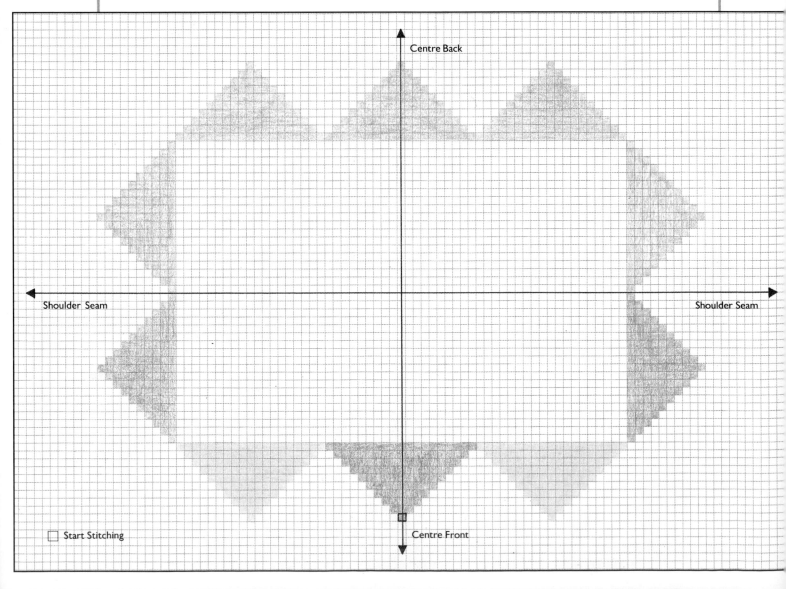

Centre Back

Shoulder Seam

Shoulder Seam

☐ Start Stitching

Centre Front

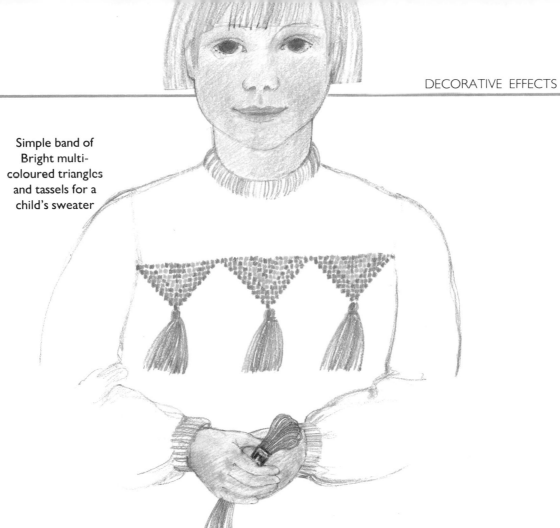

Simple band of Bright multi-coloured triangles and tassels for a child's sweater

9 Using approximately thirty 15cm (6in) lengths of yarn, make tassels as shown in the Basic Instructions. Attach one to the point of each triangle, placing green tassels on the yellow triangles, pink on the mauve, blue on the peach and peach on the blue: and finally, mauve tassels on the pink triangles and yellow on the green.

DOLL'S T-SHIRT

1 Use the same canvas as for the child's garment, but work over every thread. Place the canvas as in Fig 2. (Canvas size: 10 x 5cm/4 x 2in.)

2 Using the same colours as the child's jumper, but only one strand of thread, work a triangle similar to that shown in the illustration. Make a multi-coloured tassel to sew onto the

point of the triangle, using approximately fifteen 7.5cm (3in) lengths of yarn.

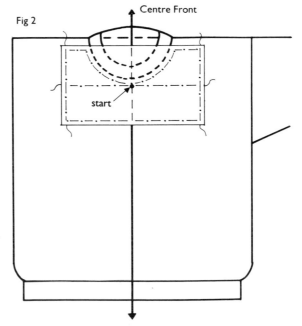

Fig 2

BEADED SWEATSHIRT
WITH HAT AND GLOVES

The inspiration for this design came from a beautiful pair of Victorian beaded knitted gloves in the Bath Museum of Costume. The original gloves were exquisitely decorated with hundreds of tiny beads; but the patterns were deceptively simple, and relied on very few colours for their effect. Gold beads had been used with the coloured ones, and these added a surprisingly subtle touch.

Here a very simple set of designs gives you the opportunity to experience this popular Victorian craft for yourself.

The glass beads are obtainable from craft shops and department stores, in larger and smaller sizes. The smaller ones are prettier, which makes them specially attractive on children's garments. But they are often more suitable for other weights of knitwear too, both on wool and cotton, as the larger beads can prove too heavy (see Basic Instructions).

GARMENT
Round-neck sweatshirt in any colour to contrast with the beads, with raglan or set-in T-shape sleeve
Knitted hat and gloves

BEADS
Glass opaque, sizes 7/0

BEADS FOR SWEATSHIRT
278 Pink beads
105 Purple beads
216 Blue beads
348 Brown beads
140 Green beads
128 Turquoise beads
Strong thread the colour of background

BEADS FOR HAT
(Beads given for 1 motif – multiply by number of motifs needed)
53 Pink beads
17 Purple beads
11 Green beads

BEADS FOR GLOVES
100 Pink beads
34 Purple beads
34 Green beads
84 Brown beads
84 Blue beads

CANVAS GAUGE
10 holes per 2.5cm (1in)

QUANTITY
24 x 18cm (9½ x 7in)

EMBROIDERED AREA (Sweatshirt)
18.5 x 12cm (7¼ x 4¾in). Bead over one double-thread of canvas (= 10 beads per 2.5cm/1in)

EMBROIDERED AREA (Gloves)
5 x 5cm (2 x 2in)

► This delicate pattern is stitched with tiny glass beads

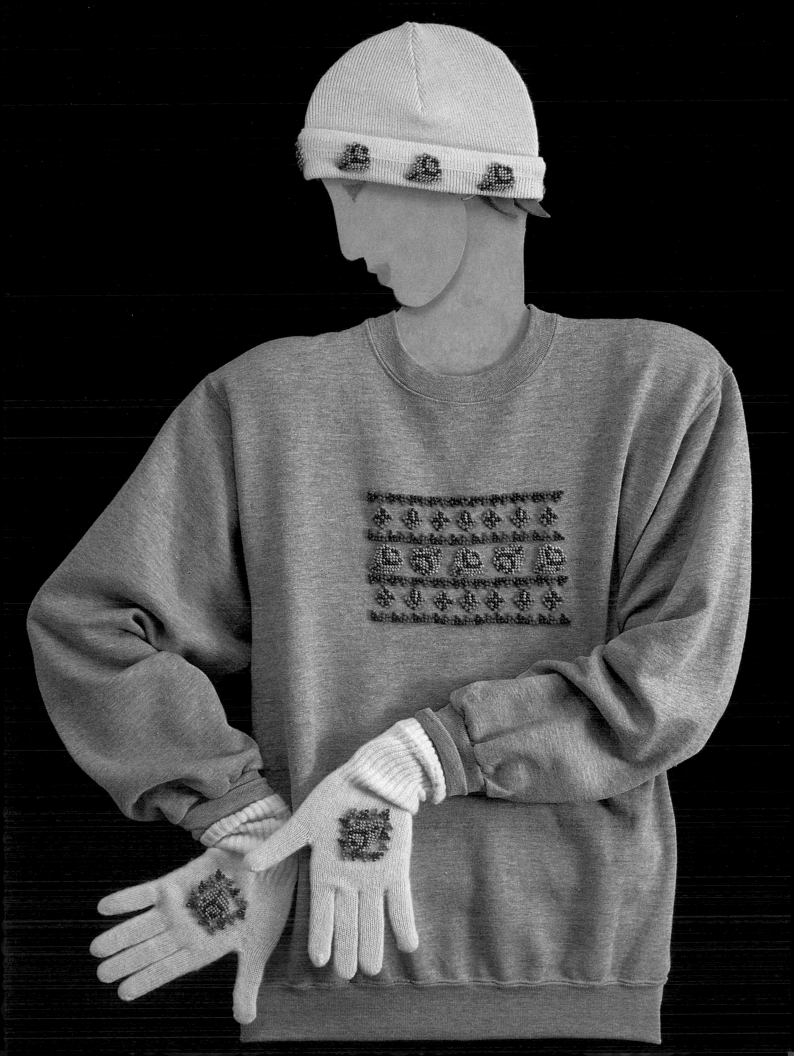

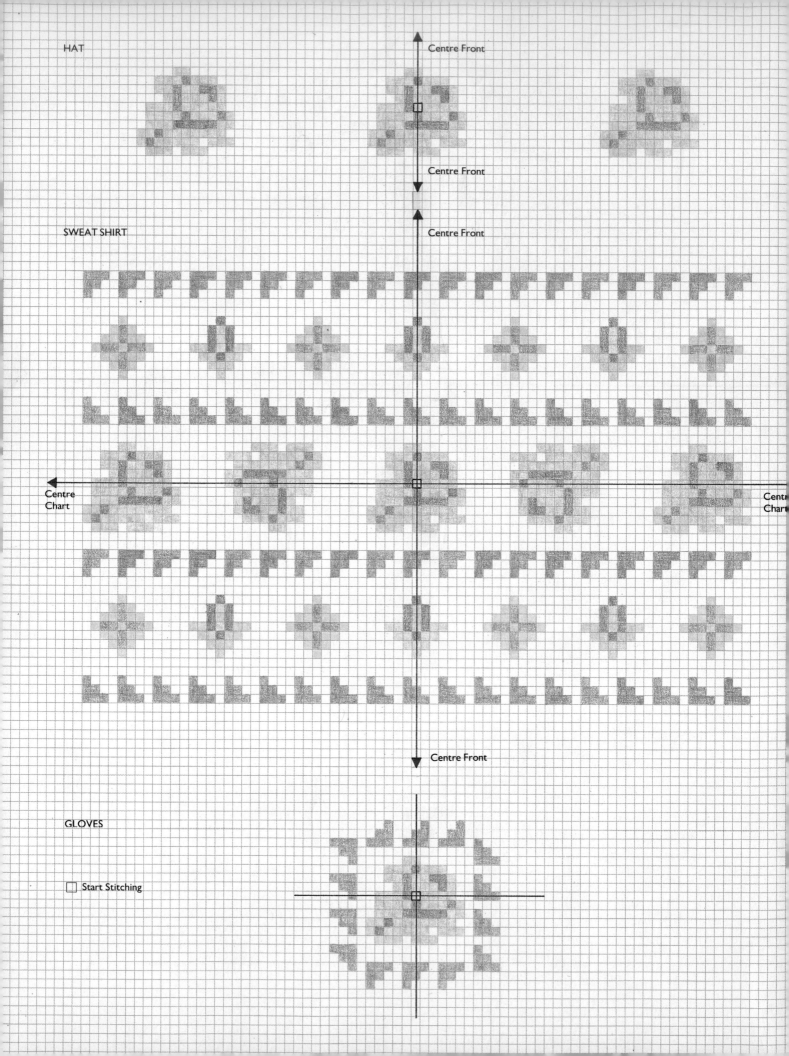

HAT

Centre Front

Centre Front

SWEAT SHIRT

Centre Front

Centre Chart

Centre Chart

Centre Front

GLOVES

☐ Start Stitching

1 Mark CF on the garment (see Basic Instructions).

2 Mark CF on the canvas (see Basic Instructions).

3 Fold the canvas across the marked line to find the centre point (see Basic Instructions).

4 Place the canvas in position as shown on Fig 1.

5 Pin and tack into place, making a grid of stitches as indicated, to secure it firmly and prevent slipping (see Basic Instructions).

6 Using strong thread, start beading at the point marked on the chart (see Basic Instructions).

7 Remove the canvas and finish as Basic Instructions.

8 To bead the hat, measure the head of the wearer.

9 Cut a piece of card to half this measurement x about 10cm (4in) deep, and fit into the hat so the ribbing is stretched (Fig 2).

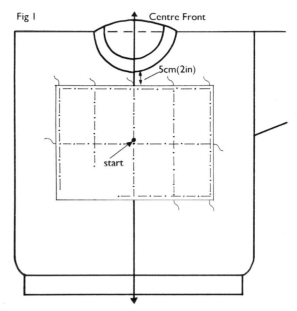

Fig 1 — Centre Front — 5cm(2in) — start

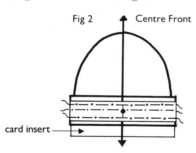

Fig 2 — Centre Front — card insert

10 Cut a piece of canvas to the length of this measurement plus an extra 5cm (2in), x approximately 8cm (3in) deep.

11 Prepare and mark CF on the canvas (Basic Instructions).

12 Fold the canvas across the marked line to find the centre point.

◄ Charts for beaded hat, sweatshirt and gloves. Each coloured square = one bead

13 Find the CF of the hat.

14 Position the canvas around the hat band as in Fig 2, overlapping the ends at CB.

15 Starting at the CF point marked on the chart, apply the beads.

16 Bead as many motifs as will fit around the hat band, spaced as indicated on the chart.

17 Remove the canvas and finish as for the sweatshirt.

18 For each glove, cut a piece of canvas 10cm (4in) square.

19 Prepare and mark the canvas (see Basic Instructions), folding it in half in both directions to find the centre point.

20 Pin and tack the canvas square onto the back of the glove, placing it centrally, and taking care to keep it aligned on the knitted fabric.

21 Start at the point marked on the chart.

22 Remove the canvas and finish as for the sweatshirt.

◄ Cross-stitch flowers and fringing in the Subtle range on a heather mix ground, creating the illusion of a shawl thrown over the shoulders

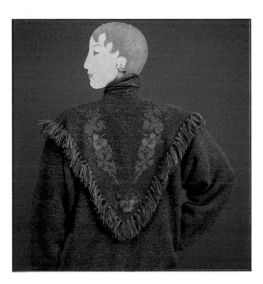

◄ The front design is repeated to form the back of the shawl collar, linked at the bottom corner by a single pansy

FLOWERED AND FRINGED CARDIGAN

This plain cardigan looks as though a shawl has been thrown over the shoulders. The simple cross-stitch design is derived from several samplers that I have designed over the years. The cottage garden flowers are placed to look like a border on the 'shawl', with the fringed edge held by fine buttonhole stitches.

The Subtle colourway melts into the heather mixture background: alternatively, work it on cream for a more defined pattern. Or, for a vibrant, folk-art effect, translate it into the Bright colourway on a black ground.

Accuracy in measuring and positioning the embroidery and fringed edge is important, so it is sensible to experiment with some of the simpler ideas before tackling this design.

The single pansy is carried onto a pair of woollen gloves. To calculate and prepare the canvas, follow the directions for the beaded gloves. Then embroider the pansy as for the central motif on the back of the cardigan, using crewel wools.

GARMENT
V-neck cardigan with T-shape set-in sleeves, of medium-gauge knitting

YARNS
Anchor Tapestry Wool (Yarn)

NUMBER OF SKEINS
Subtle Range:

8508 x 6	Pink	8044 x 4	Ochre
8608 x 5	Blue	8548 x 6	Mauve
9600 x 4	Rust	9020 x 5	Green

Chart for flowered
and fringed cardigan.
The single pansy from
the back of the
garment is repeated
on the gloves, using
a finer gauge of canvas

Centre Canvas

☐ Start Stitching

Centre Canvas

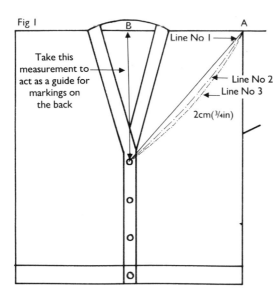

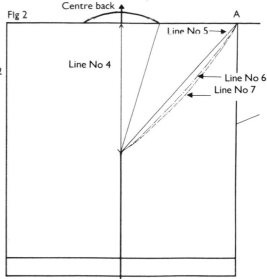

CANVAS GAUGE
8 holes per 2.5cm (1in)

QUANTITY
4 pieces 33 x 14.5cm (13 x 5¾in)
1 piece 10cm (4in) square

STITCH SIZE
8 stitches to 2.5cm (1in)

EMBROIDERED AREA
28 x 9.5cm (11 x 3¾in) x 2 = Front
36 x 36cm (14½ x 14½in) = Back

FRINGE LENGTH
Approximately 7cm (2¾in)

I Fasten the cardigan and lay it out flat (Fig 1).

2 Draw a line (line 1), using a water-soluble pen or tailors' chalk, from the sleeve head (A) to the first button.

3 Find the centre point of line 1 and mark a point 2cm (¾in) below it.

4 Draw or tack line 2 – from the button to the sleeve head (A), curving it to pass through the 2cm (¾in) mark.

5 Draw or tack line 3, 5mm (¼in) below line 2, to act as a guide for the buttonhole stitch.

6 Repeat this on the other side, double-checking to ensure that the lines of the 'shawl' curve equally on either side.

7 Make a note of the measurement from point B to the first button.

8 To prepare the back of the garment, mark in the CB, from the neck rib to the bottom rib (Fig 2). (See Basic Instructions.)

9 Taking the distance measured on the front from point B to the first button, measure down the CB to point C, and mark.

10 Draw or tack line 5 from (C) to the sleeve head (A) and repeat the same procedure as for the front (steps 3-6).

II Draw or tack line 8, from the neck rib to (C).

12 Prepare and mark the canvas placing it on front of cardigan for embroidery at each side (Fig 3 overleaf). (See Basic Instructions.)

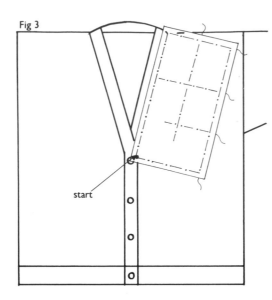

Fig 3

start

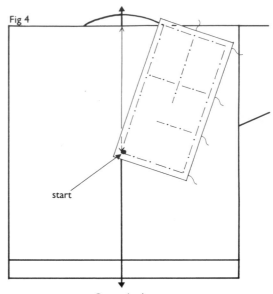

Fig 4

start

Centre back

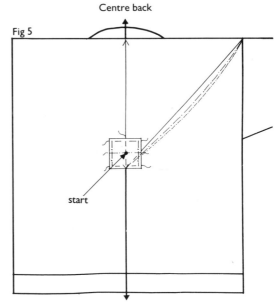

Fig 5

start

13 Mark a line all round the canvas, 2.5cm (1in) in from the edges.

14 Using the drawn line as your guide, place a corner on the junction of the neck band and the shoulder seam, and with that securely pinned, run the marked line down the neck ribbing where it joins the knitting.

15 Pin and tack into position, making a grid of stitches to secure the canvas and prevent slipping.

16 Repeat on the other side.

17 Embroider the designs, starting at the point marked on the chart, 2.5cm (1in) up, and 2.5cm (1in) in from the edge of the canvas.

18 Remove the canvas threads. (See Basic Instructions.)

19 For the back (Fig 4), follow steps 12 and 13 for the front.

20 Place the prepared canvas so that the marked line lies along line 8 and the marked corner of the canvas is on the junction of the neck band and shoulder seam.

21 Pin and tack into position, making a grid of stitches to secure firmly and prevent slipping.

22 Embroider the design, starting at the point marked on the chart, 2.5cm (1in) up and 2.5cm (1in) in from the edge of the canvas.

23 Remove the canvas threads, as before.

24 To complete the back, prepare and mark the small 10cm (4in) square of canvas in the usual way, finding

A tasselled yoke has pansies in each corner embroidered in the Bright range, whilst the child's cardigan is stitched on a larger-gauge canvas in the Pastel range

the centre point by folding it in half both ways.

25 Place the canvas for the final pansy as in Fig 5, to link the design at the back, with the CB bottom edge matched to point C on CB marked on the garment.

26 Embroider, starting at the point marked on the chart.

27 Remove the canvas threads as before.

28 To prepare for the fringe, work buttonhole stitch (see Basic Instructions), using a yarn the same colour as the garment. Place the continuous edge of the stitch on lines 3 and 7; use lines 2 and 6 as a guide for the depth of the stitch, and work each stitch approximately 12-13mm (½in) apart.

29 Cut the skeins of yarn at both ends, making 15cm (6in) lengths.

Blending one strand of each colour (six strands in all), make a fringe through every other stitch of the buttonholed line. (See Basic Instructions.)

SAMPLERS

Before the introduction of printed pattern books, samplers were made as a personal record of designs intended for embroidery on clothes and household linen. The earliest examples that are still in existence date from the early sixteenth century, and were made by privileged women of wealthy leisured families, for whom embroidery formed an important part of life.

The embroiderer added new patterns whenever she found them, placing the designs close together in a 'spot' formation, on a roll of fabric kept in her workbox for future reference. Motifs ranged from flowers, fruit and animals to emblems, knots and abstract tile patterns, many of them symbolic.

By the seventeenth century alphabets were appearing, as these were necessary for monogramming everything from underwear and bed linen to handkerchieves and purses. Needlework was an essential skill for all women, so that stitching the alphabets and repeating pattern designs also provided an effective method of teaching children and servants alike both embroidery and their letters and numbers. The colourful samplers, many of which have survived to this day, were signed and dated to record the child's progress, often from the age of seven.

The more advanced samplers from older children feature pictures and verses. Many of these pictorial samplers were so attractive that in the eighteenth century it became fashionable to embroider elaborate and very personal compositions, purely for decoration. They showed that the young ladies had been well educated. American samplers of this type are particularly lively, with houses and places depicted to record local and family history.

Throughout the nineteenth century, all classes of society in both Europe and America used samplers as a major means of educating children, in the belief that 'what was learnt by heart stayed longer in the head'. Even maps and multiplication tables were embroidered. Today sampler making is popular again, many people designing their own as mementoes recording special family events and occasions. The traditional motifs are still favourites – and often make excellent subjects to decorate knitwear.

◄ Child's sweatshirt embroidered with a
simple alphabet

ALPHABET SWEATSHIRTS
WITH HAT AND GLOVES

Take your pick from three alphabets, copied from samplers worked in previous centuries, and very different in character. Your choice depends on the purpose and situation in which you plan to use the letters or numbers. The two decorative alphabets are both nineteenth-century designs. They would make elegant initials on a sweater, or names on team or membership sweatshirts.

The simplest one is very traditional, and ideal for writing short phrases, or signing and dating your work in true sampler fashion. Two traditional ways in which you could sign your name would be to prefix it with 'wrought by' – or follow it with 'her work'. Use the graph paper at the back of the book to spell out the names or words, so that you can calculate the spacing between the letters before you begin stitching.

The child's sweatshirt embroidered with a simple alphabet is a good exercise in working out the design for your own personal name or message. Compare the photograph with the chart, and you will see that the name and date have been omitted from the chart, ready for you to insert your own information.

At the back of the book you will find examples of graph paper corresponding to the gauges of canvas that are used in the book. Select the appropriate size and, copying the charted alphabet, spell out the name on the paper. For example, JANET.

Study the letters to make sure that they are attractively spaced. Because all

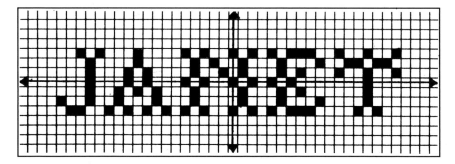

Use the graph paper to plan out the lettering
for the child's names

► Alphabets for the family: classic initials for
Father, flowers for Mother and a sampler
for Maisie

the letters are different shapes, regular spacing between every pair of letters doesn't always produce a result that is altogether pleasing to the eye. The gap between some letters will appear to be greater than elsewhere. For example: there is one space between every pair of letters except the J and A, which have been moved closer together in order to produce a more satisfactory result.

Once you are happy with your arrangement, count the number of squares in the name, including the spaces. Then halve it. In the example, the number of squares used is 36, half of which is 18. This means that the centre of the word falls on a line, whilst the centre of the design falls on a square. When this happens, simply move the centre mark to the square on the right of the line, and dot in your CF. Although technically off-centre, it won't notice after the canvas has been removed.

Return to the main chart and colour in your name, working from the CF outwards. Alternatively, you could cut out or trace the name from your own chart, and place it over the chart in the book, matching the CF lines. Fill in any available space at each side with the diamond pattern, as illustrated.

Work out the placing of the appropriate date in exactly the same way.

You will notice that the colours of the numbers, letters and diamonds run in a repeating pattern:

Red/Blue/Orange/Purple/Green/Pink/Yellow/Red/Blue, working from left to right. After the words 'made for', the diamonds continue the sequence into and through the name, and onto the right-hand diamonds and the date, so the colour of your first letter will depend on the length of the name.

On the other hand, you could simply embroider the name and date in your, or the child's favourite colour. In fact, the whole chart would look just as interesting if it was all one colour, or each line a different colour. Easier, though not so much fun to work.

Follow the same procedure to use the two other alphabets, placing the charts that you have designed in any position you like. You may find that working with Hobby Graph Paper (see Basic Instructions) will help you to space the letters and organise your designs more clearly.

CHILD'S ALPHABET SWEATSHIRT

GARMENT
Child's sweatshirt, round neck, preferably set-in T-shape sleeves

YARN
Anchor Stranded Cotton (floss). Use three strands only. Separate strands, then put them together again, before threading your needle.

NUMBER OF SKEINS

46 x 2	Red
307 x 2	Yellow
410 x 2	Blue
188 x 2	Green
112 x 2	Purple
332 x 1	Orange
40 x 1	Pink

CANVAS GAUGE
14 holes per 2.5cm (1in)

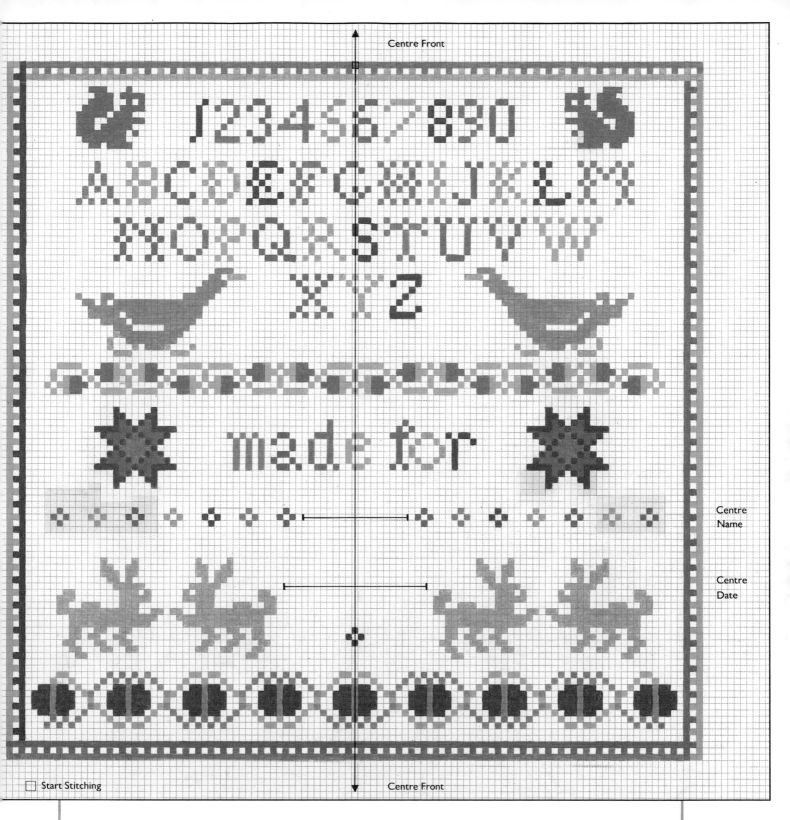

Start Stitching

Chart for child's alphabet sweatshirt with
spaces left for the appropriate name and
date. The instructions tell you how to add
your own details

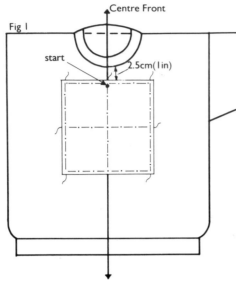

Fig 1
Centre Front
start
2.5cm(1in)

QUANTITY
24 x 24cm (9½ x 9½in)

STITCH SIZE
14 stitches per 2.5cm (1in)

EMBROIDERED AREA
Approximately 19.5 x 19cm (7¾ x 7½in)

1 Following the Basic Instructions, tack in the CF line on the garment. *Note*: On sweatshirts there is no need to take any measurements, as it is a very stable fabric.
2 Prepare and tape the canvas, marking CF as the Basic Instructions.
3 Following Fig 1, place the top edge of the canvas on the front of the sweater, with CFs matching, 2.5cm (1in) from the bottom edge of the neck rib.
4 Pin and tack in position.
5 To embroider, work the top row of colour, starting at the CF position, 2.5cm (1in) below the top edge of the canvas, as marked on the chart.
6 Finish as Basic Instructions.

LETTERED HAT AND GLOVES
GARMENT
Knitted hat and gloves

YARN
Anchor Tapestry Wool (Yarn)

NUMBER OF SKEINS
9028 x 2 Green 8440 x 1 Blue
8594 x 1 Purple 9602 x 1 Orange
8046 x 2 Yellow 8426 x 1 Red
(Includes amounts for green and yellow lettering and multi-coloured bobble)

CANVAS GAUGE
8 holes per 2.5cm (1in)

QUANTITY
One piece 5 x 46cm (2 x 18in) for the hat (approximate measurement, according to head size)
Two pieces 6.5 x 6.5cm (2½ x 2½in) for the gloves

STITCH SIZE
8 stitches per 2.5cm (1in)

APPROXIMATE LETTER SIZE
2cm (¾in) high

1 The band on the hat reads: THIS HAT BELONGS TO .... Using the 8 squares per 2.5cm (1in) graph paper supplied at the back of the book, and the basic alphabet, chart out the whole phrase, adding the name that you require.
2 Count the number of squares for the whole phrase (including the spaces), and halve this to find the CF line.
3 Measure the head of the wearer.
4 Cut a piece of card to half this

measurement x about 10cm (4in) deep, and fit it inside.

5 Before cutting your canvas, check that the length of the name won't make your charted phrase too long. If it is, cut a larger piece of card to stretch the hat further, and make sure that the phrase will now fit.

6 Cut a piece of canvas to the same length as the card, plus an extra 5cm (2in), by approximately 8cm (3in) deep.

7 Prepare and mark the canvas (see Basic Instructions).

8 Fold the canvas in half both ways and mark this line to establish the centre point.

9 Find the CF of the hat.

10 Pin and tack the canvas onto the hat, matching up the CF lines.

11 Start stitching at the central point calculated on your chart and on the canvas.

12 Finish as the Basic Instructions.

13 To embroider matching initials on the gloves, chart the letters onto the same 8 squares to 2.5cm (1in) graph paper.

14 Cut a piece of canvas to this size plus an extra 2.5cm (1in) all round.

15 Prepare and mark the canvas (see Basic Instructions), folding it in half in both directions to find the centre point.

16 Pin and tack the canvas onto the back of the glove, placing it centrally, and taking care to keep it aligned to the knitting.

17 Start stitching at the central point calculated on your charted letters and on the canvas.

18 Finish as the Basic Instructions.

19 Using multi colours of yarn make large bobble as in Basic Instructions.

MAN'S ALPHABET SWEATSHIRT

CANVAS
12 holes per 2.5cm (1in)

YARN
Anchor Stranded Cotton (floss)
(Use three strands: separate the strands, then put them together again before threading your needle)

COLOURS
308 Yellow
339 Orange

APPROXIMATE LETTER SIZE
7.5 x 7.5cm (3 x 3in)

WOMAN'S ALPHABET SWEATSHIRT

CANVAS
12 holes per 2.5cm (1in)

YARN
Anchor Stranded Cotton (floss)
Use three strands (see above)

COLOURS
268 Green
339 Rust
10 Pink
8 Pale Pink
306 Yellow
305 Pale Yellow

APPROXIMATE LETTER SIZE
4 x 5cm (1½ x 2in)

Large alphabet for a
man's sweatshirt

Pretty floral alphabet
for a woman's name

BRISTOL SWEATERS

Garments for every member of the family are embroidered with fascinating bands of pattern. These originate from the work of children educated in a group of orphanages in the English city of Bristol. Thirty-five years after the 'Muller Homes' were founded in 1836 by a German minister, over two thousand children were being taught skills that would prepare them for a working life outside the institution.

The Bristol samplers are unique: no two are identical, but all share the same alphabets and numbers in ever decreasing sizes, with simple banded and corner designs surrounding a Bible. The colour was invariably red, with occasional touches of blue.

Here, my Bristol designs include a very easy piece of embroidery for a man's sweater, consisting of six different pattern bands, which is repeated on the back. There are charted patterns to create corners for a yoke, and a multi-coloured set is illustrated for a man, woman and child.

MAN'S BRISTOL SWEATER
GARMENT
Round or V-necked sweater of medium to heavy knitwear
(Colours can be any strong contrast to the background)

YARN
Anchor Tapestry Wool (Yarn)

NUMBER OF SKEINS
8204 x 12 Red

CANVAS GAUGE
12 holes per 2.5cm (1in)

QUANTITY
Two pieces 30 x 58cm (12 x 23in)

STITCH SIZE
6 stitches per 2.5cm (1in)
(Embroider over every other hole)

EMBROIDERED AREA BACK AND FRONT
25 x 51cm (10 x 20in)

1 Open the side seams from the hem to halfway down the sleeve.
2 Following the Basic Instructions, tack the CF and CB lines, and make a note of the relevant measurements.
3 Tack in a line from underarm to underarm across the front and back.
4 Prepare and tape the canvas as directed in the Basic Instructions.
5 Fold the canvas in half lengthways to find the centre, and mark.
6 Position the canvas on the front of the garment as Fig 1 (overleaf).
7 Pin and tack into position.
8 Position the canvas on the back of the garment as in Fig 2 (overleaf), taking care to align the bottom corners of the front and back canvases at the side seams, so that the bands will be in matching positions when viewed from the side.

▶ Fascinating bands of pattern, based on nineteenth-century samplers embroidered by Bristol orphans

▲ All the family can have different patterns, using separate bands from the Bristol samplers

▼ Chart for the man's Bristol sweater. Repeat the entire chart on the back (see canvas placing diagram)

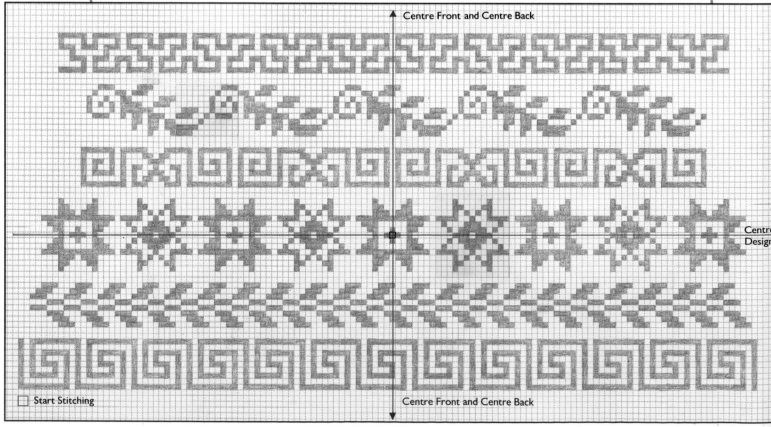

Centre Front and Centre Back

Centre Design

☐ Start Stitching

Centre Front and Centre Back

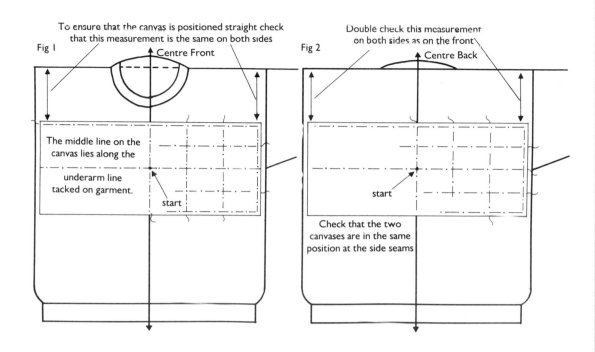

Fig 1

To ensure that the canvas is positioned straight check that this measurement is the same on both sides

Centre Front

The middle line on the canvas lies along the

underarm line tacked on garment.

start

Fig 2

Double check this measurement on both sides as on the front

Centre Back

start

Check that the two canvases are in the same position at the side seams

9 Pin and tack into position.
Note: As it is a large canvas, make a grid of tacking stitches over it to hold it in place and prevent slipping (see Basic Instructions).

10 Working the cross stitch over every other hole of the canvas, start to embroider the front on the CF line, in the middle of the central star at the point shown on the chart.

11 Embroider the back as directed for the front.

12 Finish as the Basic Instructions.

WOMAN'S BRISTOL SWEATSHIRT
GARMENT
Round neck sweatshirt, raglan or set-in T-shape sleeves in a strong colour to contrast with bright embroidery

YARN
Anchor Stranded Cotton (floss) (Use four strands: separate the individual strands, then place together again before threading the needle)

APPROXIMATE NUMBER OF SKEINS
316 x 1	Orange
88 x 4	Pink
111 x 5	Purple
303 x 4	Gold
245 x 3	Green
132 x 1	Blue

CANVAS GAUGE
12 holes per 2.5cm (1in)

QUANTITY
24 x 40.5cm (9½ x 16in)

STITCH SIZE
12 stitches per 2.5cm (1in)

APPROXIMATE EMBROIDERED AREA
Front: 19 x 35.5cm (7½ x 14in)
Back: 14 x 35.5cm (5½ x 14in)

Centre Front and Centre Back

Multi-coloured charted yoke in cottons for
the woman's Bristol sweatshirt

HEARTS AND FLOWERS SWEATER

The Heart and Basket of Flowers is a favourite subject, seen here worked in strong colours, with a carnation, tulip, pansy and honeysuckle. There are hearts on each sleeve, and I have repeated the basket on the back.

For children and adults alike, the flowers look very pretty when growing out of a heart and up a cardigan in softer, more subtle shades. Or flowers in similar muted colours could be worked in a repeating band formation. Simply calculate the size of stitch and canvas gauge needed for your chosen garment.

GARMENT
Any round-necked, long- or short-sleeved garment
(This design could also be worked in six-stranded cotton onto a sweatshirt)
Other coloured grounds: navy, brown, grey, very pale pastels, white or beige

YARNS
Anchor Tapestry Wool (Yarn)

NUMBER OF SKEINS
8664 x 1   Orange
8136 x 2   Yellow
9200 x 3   Green
8596 x 2   Purple
8608 x 2   Blue
8348 x 2   Deep Pink
8346 x 2   Pink

CANVAS GAUGE
12 holes per 2.5cm (1in)

QUANTITY
A piece 18 x 15cm (7 x 6in) for each motif

STITCH SIZE
6 stitches per 2.5cm (1in)
(Embroider over every other hole)

EMBROIDERED AREA
Front: 42 x 42cm (16½ x 16½in)
Back: 11 x 10cm (4½ x 4in)
Sleeves: 9 x 10cm (3½ x 4in)
Note: These areas can be adjusted very easily by slightly rearranging the separate canvases.

1 Open the side seams from the hems to the cuffs. Lay the jumper flat.
2 Following the Basic Instructions, mark the CF and CB lines, and also the centre of the sleeve (CS).
3 On the front of the garment, measure the shoulder seams from the neck rib to the sleeve head: at the halfway points mark and tack a vertical line down the garment to the rib (see Fig 1 overleaf).
4 Prepare and tape the separate pieces of canvas as Basic Instructions.
5 Fold each canvas in half horizontally to find centre, and mark the line.
6 Place the separate pieces of canvas on the front of the sweater, as shown in Fig 1. Pin and tack through the centre of each, and then around the outside edges. *Note*: Make sure that the centres of the four outside sections of canvas are aligned: check these measurements by measuring from the centre of each canvas to the shoulder seam.

continued on p76

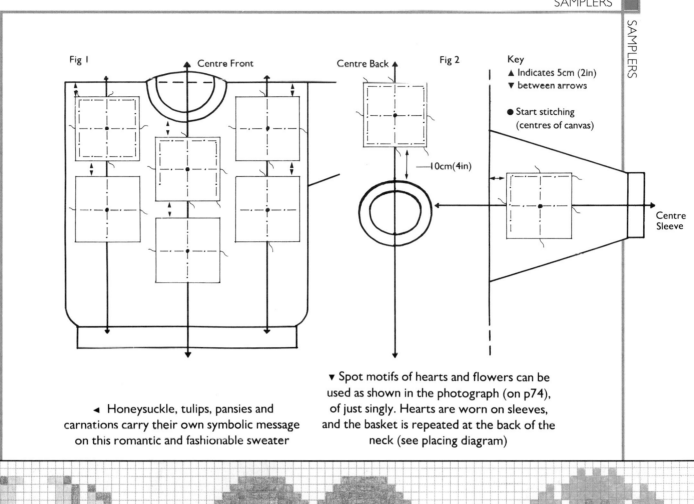

Fig I
Centre Front

Centre Back

Fig 2

Key
▲ Indicates 5cm (2in)
▼ between arrows

● Start stitching
(centres of canvas)

—10cm(4in)

Centre Sleeve

▼ Spot motifs of hearts and flowers can be used as shown in the photograph (on p74), of just singly. Hearts are worn on sleeves, and the basket is repeated at the back of the neck (see placing diagram)

◄ Honeysuckle, tulips, pansies and carnations carry their own symbolic message on this romantic and fashionable sweater

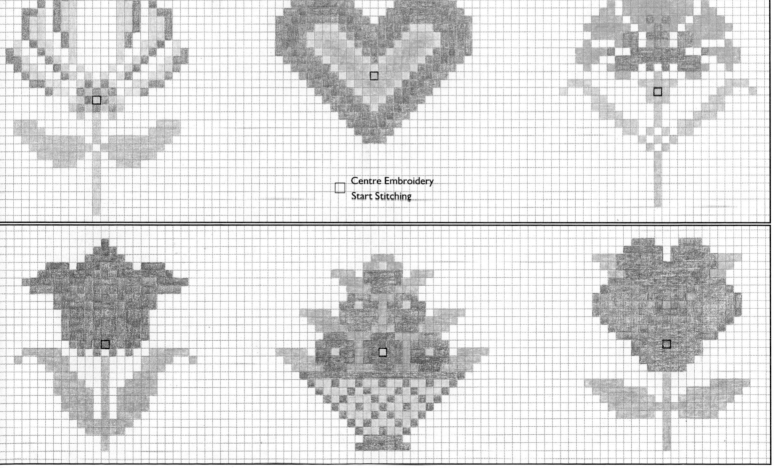

Centre Embroidery
Start Stitching

7 Find the centre stitch of each design (see chart), and embroider outwards, working over every other hole of the canvas.

8 On the back of the sweater, pin and tack the canvas into position as shown in Fig 2.

9 Working over every other hole of the canvas, embroider the basket of flowers, following the chart.

10 On the sleeves, pin and tack canvas into position, as shown in Fig 2.

11 Embroider the hearts, following the chart.

12 Finish as Basic Instructions.

HEARTS AND FLOWERS CARDIGAN

GARMENT
Round-necked button-through cardigan
(The design would look good on any dark grounds, pale greys, creams and pastels)

YARNS
Anchor Tapestry Wool (Yarn)

APPROXIMATE NUMBER OF SKEINS
8506 x 1   Pink
8508 x 1   Deep Pink
9510 x 1   Orange
9512 x 1   Rust
8548 x 1   Mauve
8550 x 1   Purple
8044 x 1   Gold
8040 x 1   Yellow
9022 x 4   Green

CANVAS GAUGE
16 holes per 2.5cm (1in)

QUANTITY
Two pieces 43 x 20cm (17 x 8in)

STITCH SIZE
8 stitches per 2.5cm (1in)
(Embroider over every other hole)

APPROXIMATE EMBROIDERED AREA
38 x 15cm (15 x 6in) x 2

► Rows of repeating flowers would be ideal for a girl's sweater

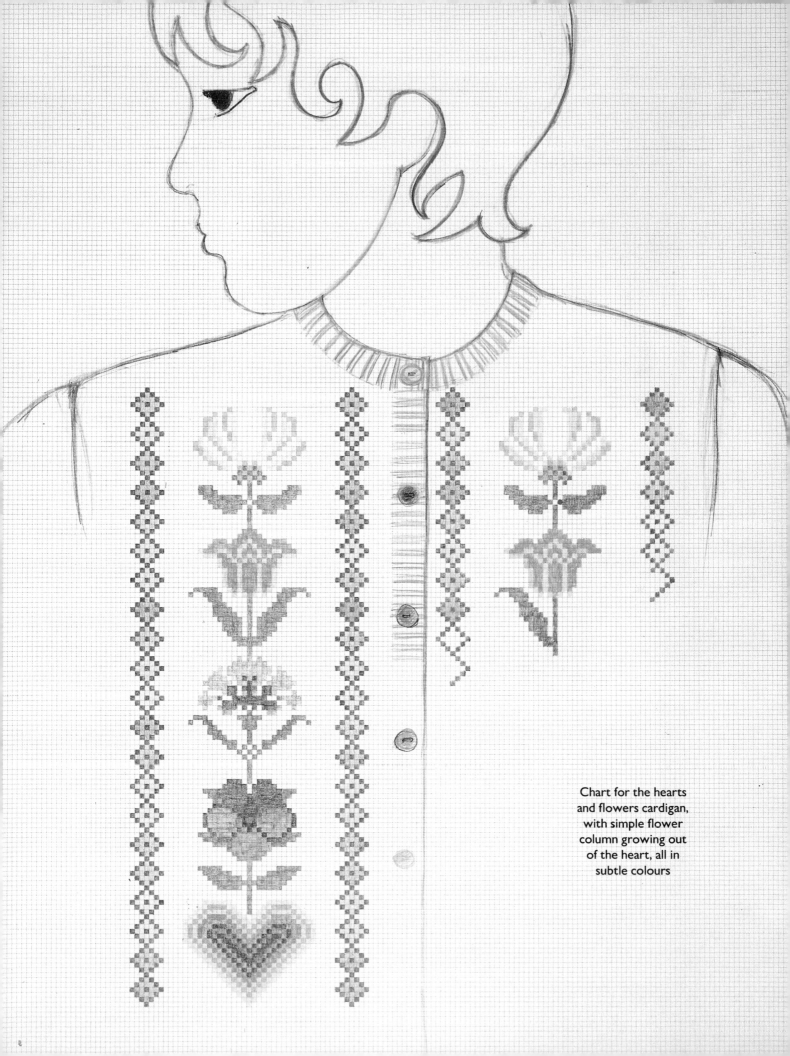

Chart for the hearts
and flowers cardigan,
with simple flower
column growing out
of the heart, all in
subtle colours

The back of the ▶
Medallions sweater
is signed in
traditional sampler
fashion

A gift ▶
embroidered by a
Quaker schoolgirl
inspired the
exquisite Medallions
design embroidered
in fine yarn on a
lambswool sweater

QUAKER MEDALLIONS SWEATER

This finely embroidered lambswool sweater is based on two samplers in the Bristol Museum, one of which is signed 'Hannah Searls – Ackworth School – 1808'. It was probably embroidered as a gift, since it is signed 'HS to MS 1808.' Ackworth boarding school was founded in Yorkshire, England in 1779 by the Quakers. Similar samplers originated in Quaker communities and boarding schools in America, notably Pennsylvania and New York.

The original samplers were worked in pastels, but this modern version makes a stronger statement, using one pale colour in a very fine yarn to contrast with the dark ground. The medallion on the back of the sweater frames your signature and date – or a dedication, if a gift. The effect of this design relies on the exquisitely fine embroidery, so it is not one to be attempted until you have some experience of working with thicker yarns on larger-gauge canvas.

My other designs show simple corner leaf motifs and a multi-coloured medallion.

GARMENT
Round- or V-necked lambswool or
fine woollen sweater, in any
colour making a good contrast with
the embroidery (Could also be
worked in silk or cotton)

YARNS
DMC Broder Medici (use two strands)

NUMBER OF SKEINS
8329 x 12 Ecru

CANVAS
12 holes per 2.5cm (1in)

QUANTITY
Two pieces 52 x 33cm (20½ x 13in)
(back and front)

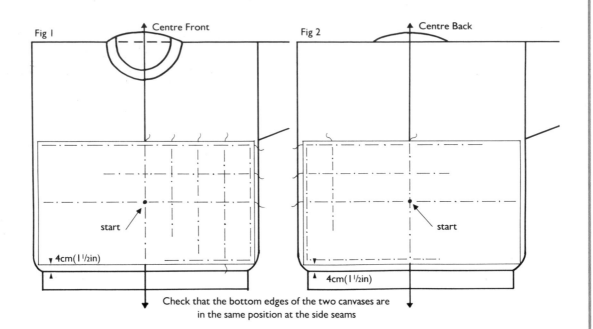

Fig 1 — Centre Front — start — 4cm(1½in)

Fig 2 — Centre Back — start — 4cm(1½in)

Check that the bottom edges of the two canvases are
in the same position at the side seams

STITCH SIZE
12 stitches per 2.5cm (1in)

EMBROIDERED AREA
45 x 26cm (18 x 10½in)
(both back and front)

1 Open the side seams of the garment from hem to underarm.

2 Following the Basic Instructions, tack in the CF and CB lines, and take the relevant measurements.

3 Prepare and tape the canvas as Basic Instructions.

4 Find and mark the centre point of both pieces of canvas by folding them in half in both directions. *Note*: Very fine woollens need great care to avoid stretching. Double check all measurements, so that the canvas is straight on the garment and the sides match evenly.

5 Position the front canvas as in Fig 1.

6 Pin and tack into position, making a grid of stitches to secure the canvas firmly and prevent it slipping (Basic Instructions).

7 Position the back canvas as in Fig 2.

8 Pin and tack into position, again making a grid of stitches over it. *Note*: Ensure that both pieces of canvas are securely tacked, so that they are aligned at the side seams, at the underarm and rib positions.

9 Using two strands of yarn in the needle, start embroidering the front at the central point marked on the chart.

10 Embroider the back in the same way, starting at the point marked on the chart.

Note: If you wish to change the wording of the back medallion, copy out the medallion outline onto the graph paper provided at the back. Then turn to the basic alphabet charted for the child's sampler sweatshirt, and letter in your own message, or initials and date.

11 Finish as Basic Instructions.

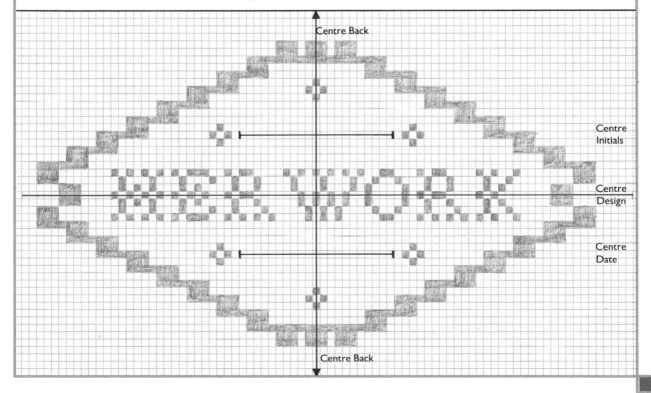

Centre Front

☐ Start Stitching

▲ Chart for the front of the Quaker design

▼ Chart for back of Quaker design, with
spaces left for your name and date. If you
don't wish to use this, omit it and embroider
just the two bands of leaves

Centre Back

Centre
Initials

Centre
Design

Centre
Date

Centre Back

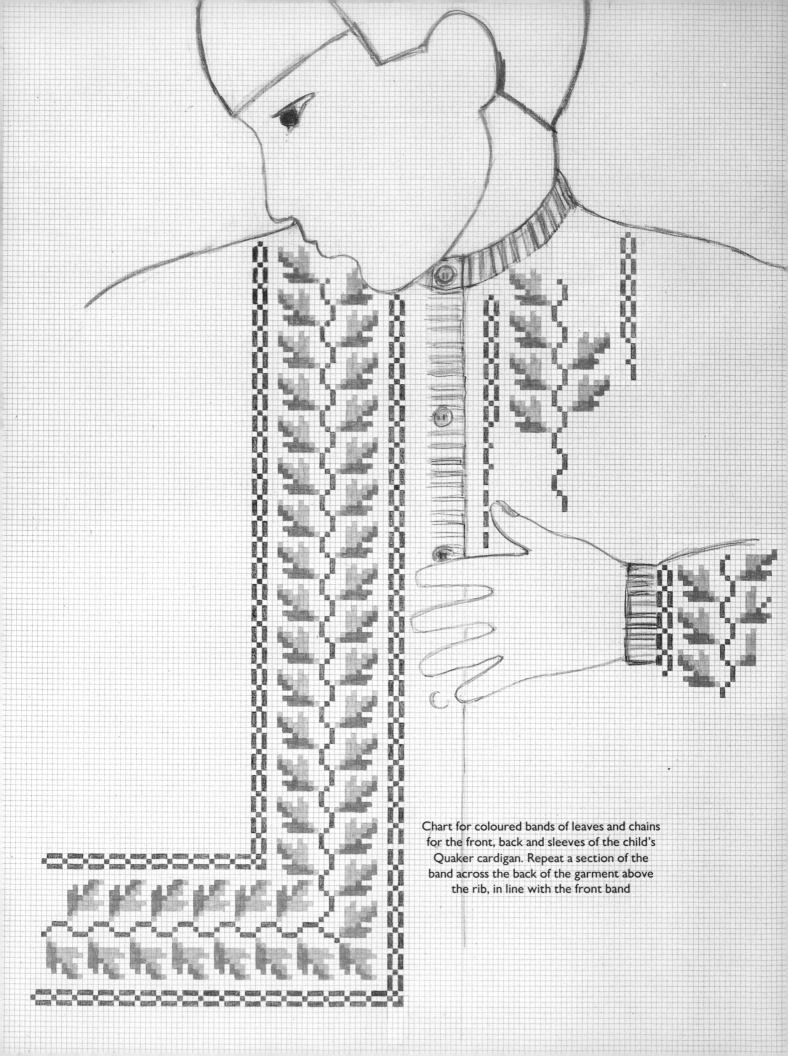

Chart for coloured bands of leaves and chains
for the front, back and sleeves of the child's
Quaker cardigan. Repeat a section of the
band across the back of the garment above
the rib, in line with the front band

CHILD'S QUAKER CARDIGAN
GARMENT
Button-to-neck fine-gauge-knit child's cardigan, with set-in T-shaped sleeves, in any good contrasting colour not used in the embroidery

YARN
DMC Broder Medici (using three strands of wool in the needle)

APPROXIMATE NUMBER OF SKEINS
8176 x 1   Rust
8899 x 7   Blue
8342 x 5   Pale Green
8346 x 5   Deep Green

CANVAS GAUGE
8 holes per 2.5cm (1in)

APPROXIMATE QUANTITY
Front: two pieces 14 x 48cm (5½ x 19in)
Sleeves: two pieces 14 x 15cm (5½ x 6in)
Back: 14 x 35.5cm (5½ x 14in)

STITCH SIZE
8 stitches per 2.5cm (1in)

APPROXIMATE EMBROIDERED AREA
Width of band: 9cm (3½in)
Length of band: 43cm (17in)
The band is repeated on the back above the rib, in line with the front band at the rib (as for the main design)

One medallion in bold colours in a large format could be used on the back of a cardigan

INTERLACE SWEATER

Strong linear patterns of bands and knots are found on the early English samplers of the sixteenth and seventeenth centuries. These intricate patterns were much used in the decoration of Tudor and Jacobean homes: on plasterwork and carved wood inside the house, and in the knot gardens outside. The same designs can be found decorating the collars and cuffs of both men's and women's undergarments. Just the outside lines were embroidered in a single colour: black, red or blue, or with gold, which was used for Royalty. In portraits of the period these garments are deliberately visible at the wrists and neck. In later samplers the outlines are filled in with different colours to make rich and varied patterns.

The man's cream Guernsey sweater shown here is in the muted shades of the early samplers. The band is repeated on the back and sleeves, and a small medallion is placed below the back neck band.

Other versions show the patterns in outline only but filled with jewel-like colours they would look striking on dark backgrounds.

GARMENT
Very firm knitting, ideally a Guernsey or fisherman's knit, with round or straight neck. The embroidery is very dense, so needs a strong ground, light-coloured or rich autumn shades, but not black

YARNS
Anchor Tapestry Wool (Yarn)

NUMBER OF SKEINS
8046 x 3	Ochre
9666 x 16	Brown
9022 x 2	Green
8740 x 10	Blue
8352 x 7	Burgundy

CANVAS GAUGE
8 holes per 2.5cm (1in)

QUANTITY
Front: one piece 38 x 50cm (15 x 20in)

Back: (band) one piece 12 x 50cm (5 x 20in); (medallion) one piece 15 x 15cm (6 x 6in)
Sleeves: two pieces 20 x 12cm (8 x 5in)

STITCH SIZE
8 stitches per 2.5cm (1in)

EMBROIDERED AREA
Front: 33 x 46cm (13 x 18in)
Back: 7 x 46cm (3 x 18in) (band)
          10 x 10cm (4 x 4in) (medallion)
Sleeves: 15 x 7.5cm (6 x 3in)

Bold geometric patterns forming bands ▶ and knots were popular in the sixteenth and seventeenth centuries, and feature prominently on the earliest samplers

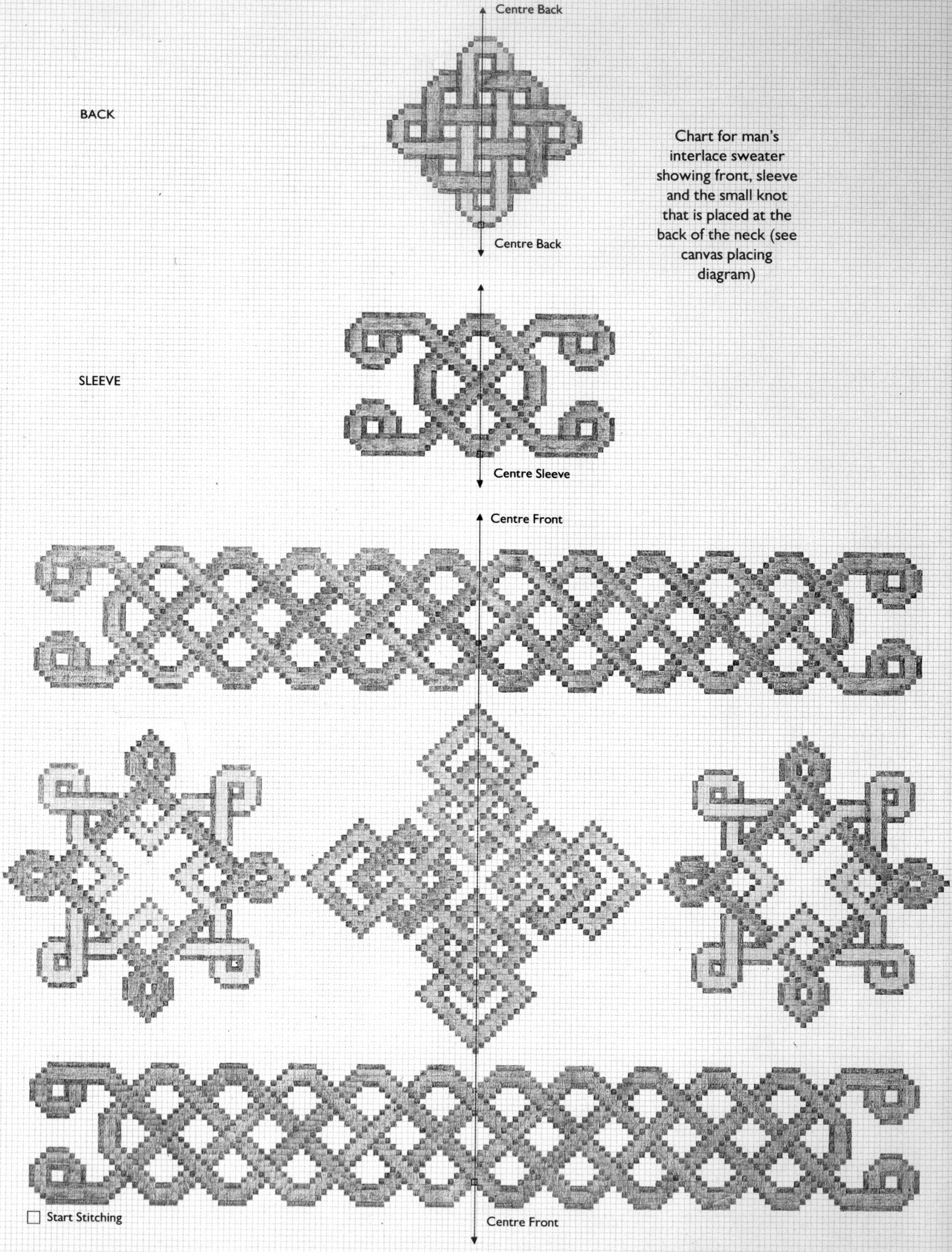
Centre Back
BACK
Centre Back
SLEEVE
Centre Sleeve
Centre Front
Start Stitching
Centre Front

Chart for man's interlace sweater showing front, sleeve and the small knot that is placed at the back of the neck (see canvas placing diagram)

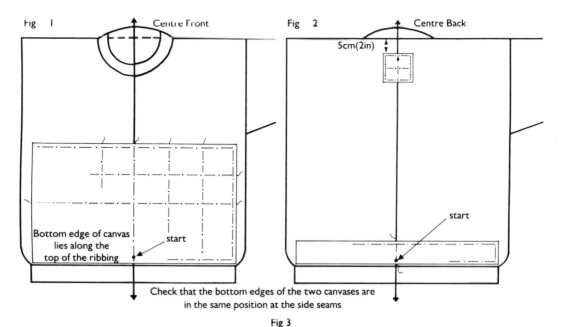

Fig 1 · Centre Front · Fig 2 · Centre Back · 5cm(2in)

Bottom edge of canvas lies along the top of the ribbing · start · start

Check that the bottom edges of the two canvases are in the same position at the side seams

Fig 3

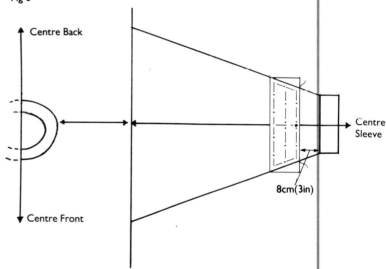

Centre Back · Centre Sleeve · Centre Front · 8cm(3in)

1 Open the side seams from the hem to underarm, and at the wrists to halfway up the sleeves. If a Guernsey is being used, try not to interfere with the intricate seaming under the arm.

2 Following the Basic Instructions, tack in the CB and CF lines, and also both CS lines.

3 Position the front canvas as in Fig 1. Pin and tack. (See Basic Instructions.)

4 Position each back canvas as Fig 2. Pin and tack.

5 Position each sleeve canvas as Fig 3. Pin and tack.

6 Make a grid of tacking stitches across the pieces of canvas to secure them firmly and prevent slipping (see Basic Instructions).

7 Start embroidering the front 2.5cm (1in) above the bottom edge of the canvas at the point shown on the chart. Work the bottom band, then the medallions and then the top band.

8 Start embroidering the back band as for the front.

9 Start working the medallion at CB, 2.5cm (1in) down from the top edge of the canvas at the point marked on the chart.

10 Start embroidering the sleeves at the bottom of the band nearest to the CS position.

11 Finish as Basic Instructions.

Outlines of medallions and knots which could be used for a man's interlace sweater, and a jewel-like yoke for a woman

WOMAN'S INTERLACE CARDIGAN

GARMENT
Round-neck button-through cardigan, with any pale ground

YARN
Anchor Tapestry Wool (Yarn)

APPROXIMATE NUMBER OF SKEINS
8626 x 1	Blue
8132 x 1	Yellow
8346 x 2	Pink
9162 x 2	Green
9800 x 4	Black

CANVAS GAUGE
10 holes per 2.5cm (1in)

QUANTITY
Two pieces 18 x 55cm (7 x 22in)

STITCH SIZE
5 stitches per 2.5cm (1in)
(Work over every other hole)

APPROXIMATE EMBROIDERED AREA
Approximately 13 x 50cm (5 x 20in)

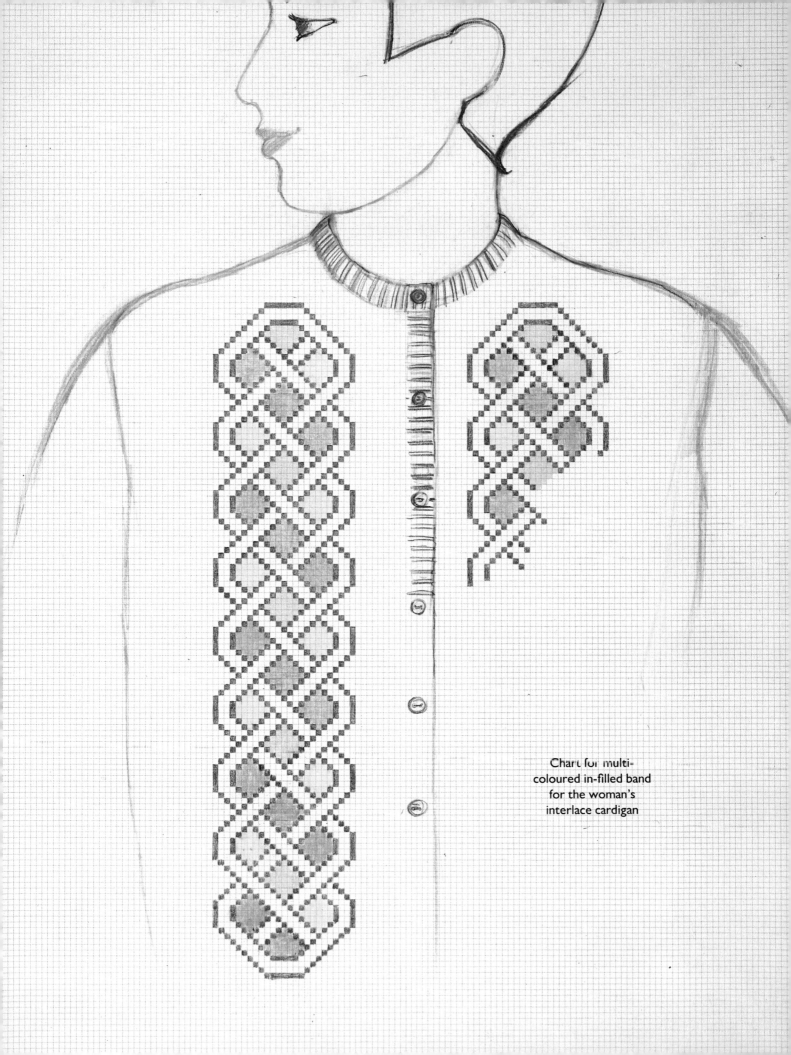

Chart for multi-
coloured in-filled band
for the woman's
interlace cardigan

CARNATIONS SWEATER

The Carnation has several guises: Pink, Dianthus, and also the Gillyflower of Medieval heraldry. In one form or another, it has been embroidered throughout the ages. For this interpretation I have combined designs from Yugoslavian, French and English samplers. The Basket of Carnations – typical of eighteenth-century English samplers – still looks fresh and pretty against a natural coloured ground. The border, and the large and small motifs, could all be used in many different ways.

Note: If you wish to scale this design down for children, use a finer crewel wool. On sweatshirts, use stranded cottons (floss) (see Basic Instructions: Adapting Designs).

GARMENT
Round-necked sweater with set-in T-shape or raglan sleeves, measuring approximately 58cm (23in) from front neck to top of ribbing. Medium to heavyweight knitwear is necessary; if garment is too loosely knitted, the small embroidery stitches will fall through the fabric. Any contrasting coloured background would be attractive, eg dark navy or black

YARNS
Anchor Tapestry Wool (Yarn)

NUMBER OF SKEINS
8628 x 3   Blue
8400 x 3   Deep Pink
9004 x 5   Green
8366 x 5   Pale Pink

CANVAS GAUGE
8 holes per 2.5cm (1in)

QUANTITY
Three separate pieces:
51 x 51cm (20 x 20in)
51 x 10cm (20 x 4in)
13 x 13cm (5 x 5in)

STITCH SIZE
8 stitches per 2.5cm (1in)

EMBROIDERED AREA
Front: 43 x 46cm (17 x 18in)
Back band: 46 x 6cm (18 x 2½in)
Individual flower: 6 x 5cm (2½ x 2in)

1   Open the side seams of the garment from hem to underarm.
2   Following the Basic Instructions, tack in the CF and CB lines from neck to hem, and make relevant measurements.
3   Prepare each piece of canvas as in the Basic Instructions, marking the CF and CB.
4   Position the front canvas as in Fig 1 (overleaf). Pin and tack. A grid of tacking stitches through both the canvas and garment will prevent any slipping and distortion of the fabric (see Basic Instructions).

Also known as Dianthus, Pink and ▶ Gillyflower, the Carnation has been a favourite flower for embroidery down the centuries. The 'Basket of Carnations' motif is a typical eighteenth-century example

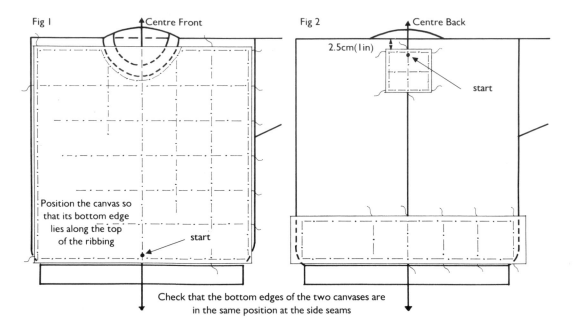

Fig 1   ↑Centre Front

Position the canvas so that its bottom edge lies along the top of the ribbing   start

Fig 2   ↑Centre Back

2.5cm(1in)   start

Check that the bottom edges of the two canvases are in the same position at the side seams

5 Position the back pieces of canvas as in Fig 2. Pin and tack.

6 Start to embroider the front at the CF point (see Fig 1) as marked on the chart.

Work the small diamond pattern first, from the centre outwards. Then continue as you like.

Note: Careful counting is necessary to ensure that the small pinks are accurately positioned in relation to each other.

7 Embroider the lower band on the back as for the front. For the individual carnation at the top, start 2.5cm (1in) below the top of the canvas, as marked on the chart (see Fig 2).

8 Finish as Basic Instructions.

CARNATION CARDIGAN (p94)

GARMENT
Button-to-neck woman's cardigan, medium-weight knitting

YARN
Anchor Tapestry Wool (Yarn)

APPROXIMATE NUMBER OF SKEINS

8608 x 4	Blue	8038 x 2	Yellow
8018 x 2	Ochre	9002 x 2	Green

CANVAS
8 holes per 2.5cm (1in)

QUANTITY
Two pieces 43 x 23cm (17 x 9in)

STITCH SIZE
8 stitches per 2.5cm (1in)

EMBROIDERED AREA
Approximately 38 x 18cm (15 x 7in) x 2. (Includes one repeat motif at back neck)

Chart for carnations sweater. Use one
single small bowed carnation at the back of
the neck, and repeat the lower bands of
diamonds and carnations on the back, above
the rib (see canvas placing diagram)

Centre Front

Centre Front

☐ Start Stitching

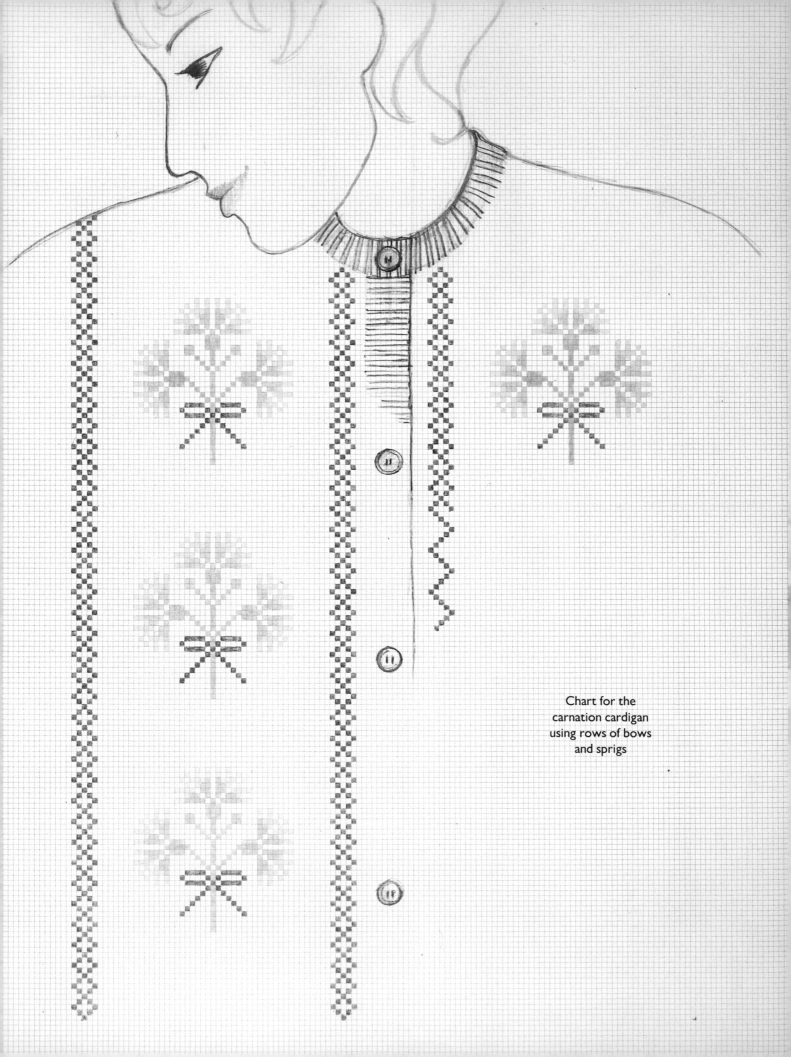

Chart for the
carnation cardigan
using rows of bows
and sprigs

Two carnation alternatives: a multi-coloured
pot of carnations, embroidered using a larger
canvas gauge for a handsome jacket, or a
prettily sprigged fine jumper or sweatshirt

FARMHOUSE AND GARDEN SWEATSHIRT

The inspiration for this set of designs comes from the samplers of America, in which many different styles converged, resulting in livelier and more individual pieces of work than English samplers of the same periods.

This design for a child's sweatshirt or T-shirt depicts a house with a farmyard in naturalistic colours. Any one of the motifs could be repeated at the back neck: here it is the sun. For mothers, there is a 'Home is where the Heart is' version, with a garden of flowering plants. The simple stylised picket fence and trees is for fathers.

GARMENT
Round-necked child's sweatshirt or T-shirt, with long or short sleeves, in any dark colour, or pastels, not included in the embroidery

YARNS
Anchor Stranded Cotton (floss) (Use four strands: separate the individual strands, then place together again before threading the needle)

NUMBER OF SKEINS
268 x 2	Green
281 x 1	Pale Green
365 x 3	Orange
907 x 2	Yellow
874 x 1	Pale Yellow
5975 x 1	Red
336 x 1	Pink
387 x 1	Cream

CANVAS GAUGE
10 holes per 2.5cm (1in)

◄ A charming pictorial design for a child's sweatshirt

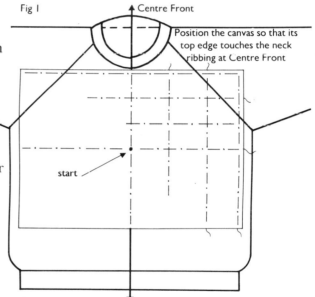

Fig 1   Centre Front

Position the canvas so that its top edge touches the neck ribbing at Centre Front

start

QUANTITY
Front: 40 x 33cm (16 x 13in)
Back: 7 x 7cm (3 x 3in)

STITCH SIZE
10 stitches per 2.5cm (1in)

EMBROIDERED AREA
Front: 36 x 26cm (14 x 10½in)
Back: 4.5 x 4.5cm (1¾ x 1¾in)

1   Measure and mark CF and CB lines on garment (see Basic Instructions).

2   Prepare and mark the pieces of canvas (see Basic Instructions).

3   Fold the canvas in half in both directions to find and mark the centre point.

4   Position the canvas on the front of the garment as in Fig 1.

5   Pin and tack into place.

6   Make a grid of stitches to hold the canvas securely and prevent it slipping (see Basic Instructions).

7   For the back, position the canvas 2.5cm (1in) below the neck rib down the CB line. (Refer to Fig 2 for the Carnation design.)

8   Pin and tack into place.

9   Start to embroider the front with the centre stitch as marked on the chart.

10   Start to embroider the back with centre stitch as marked on chart.

11   Finish as Basic Instructions.

Chart for child's farmhouse and garden sweatshirt, with assorted animals

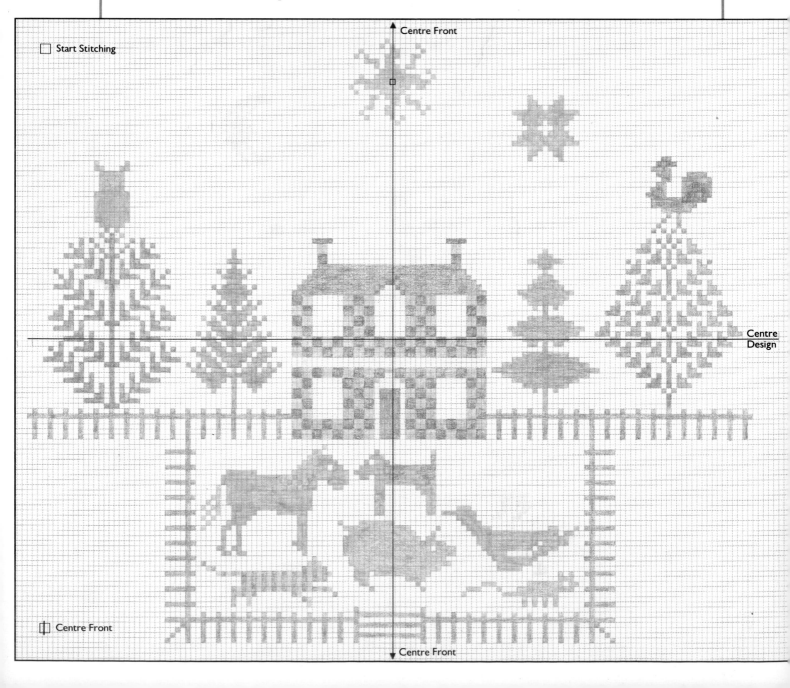

Start Stitching

Centre Front

Centre Design

Centre Front

Centre Front

HOUSE AND GARDEN WOMAN'S SWEATSHIRT

GARMENT

Sweatshirt, raglan or set-in T-shape sleeves, in any neutral or dark ground not included in the embroidery

YARN

Anchor Stranded Cotton (floss) (Use four strands: separate the individual strands, then place them together again before threading the needle)

APPROXIMATE NUMBER OF SKEINS

121 x 2	Blue
336 x 1	Pink
874 x 1	Yellow
907 x 1	Ochre
268 x 2	Mid Green
281 x 2	Light Green

For father, a row of evergreen trees and a fence decorate a simple sweater

218 x 2	Dark Green
5975 x 1	Dark Pink
365 x 3	Orange
387 x 1	Cream

CANVAS

10 holes per 2.5cm (1in)

QUANTITY

50 x 35cm (20½ x 14½in)

STITCH SIZE

10 stitches per 2.5cm (1in)

APPROXIMATE EMBROIDERED AREA

Approximately 47 x 32cm (18½ x 12½in)

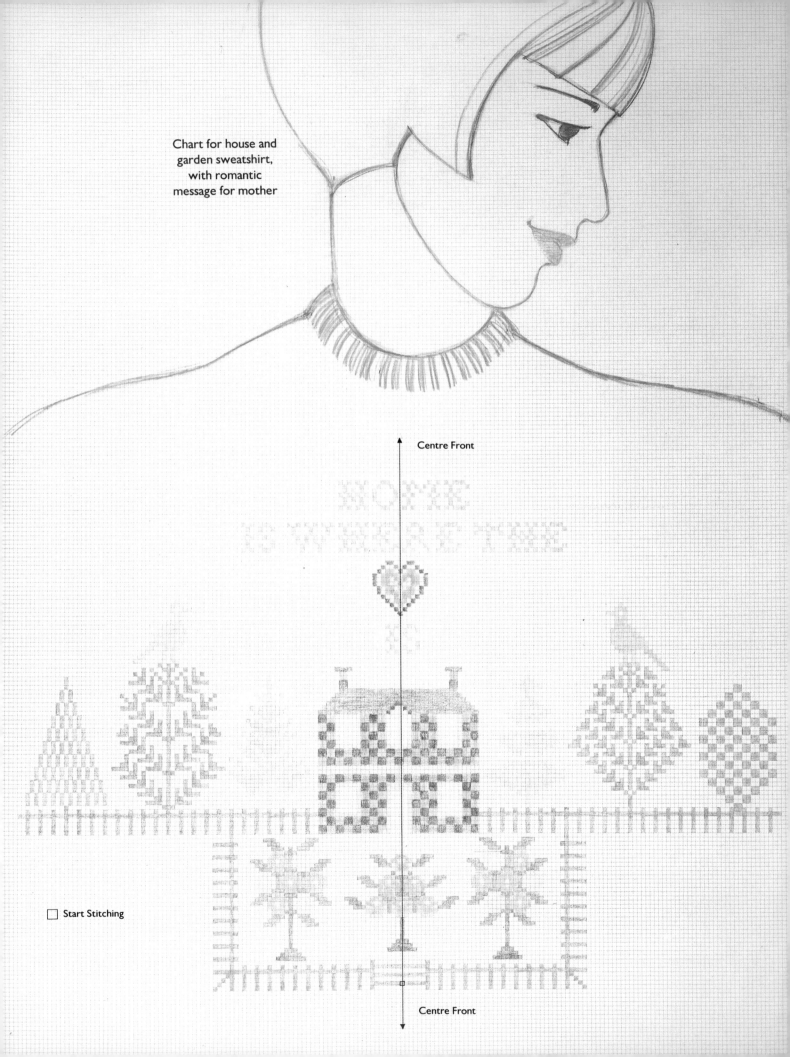

Chart for house and
garden sweatshirt,
with romantic
message for mother

Centre Front

□ Start Stitching

Centre Front

TREE AND STAGS SWEATER

This tree is adapted from a sampler dated 1598. The pelican watching over her young represents Dutifulness, whilst the squirrels symbolise Mischief. The elegant stags are thought to be Swedish. The bottom band is repeated on the back of the garment, and the bird reappears below the neck band – or it could be a squirrel.

The variations developed from these motifs make amusing bands and borders. The children's banded chart might be stitched in crewel wool onto a sweater, or with cottons onto a sweatshirt. The large stags would look handsome with the leaf border on a cardigan.

These designs need careful counting, so it would be wise to wait until you have worked some of the simpler examples before attempting this one.

GARMENT

Round neck, long or short sweater with set-in T-shape or raglan sleeves, measuring 58cm (23in) or more from neck to top of ribbing. Medium- to heavy-weight knitwear; a firmly knitted fabric is necessary to prevent the small embroidery stitches falling through a loosely knitted ground. The design would be equally effective on black, navy or beige

YARNS

Anchor Tapestry Wool (Yarn)

NUMBER OF SKEINS

9564 x 4	Rust
8046 x 1	Dark Yellow
9526 x 7	Orange
9600 x 3	Pink
8044 x 3	Yellow
9642 x 3	Brown
9202 x 7	Green

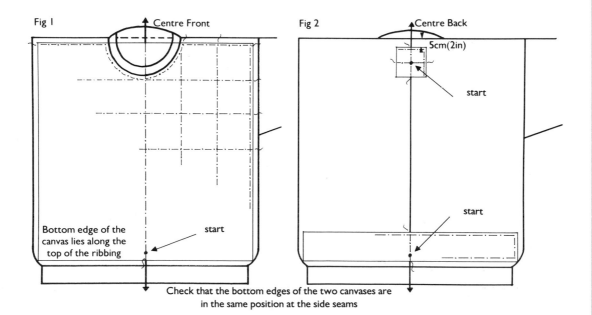

Check that the bottom edges of the two canvases are in the same position at the side seams

◄ The tree, with its 'dutiful' mother pelican and 'mischievous' squirrels, is adapted from a very old sampler of 1598. The elegant stags are thought to be Swedish

▼ Tree and stags chart. The squirrel band is repeated on the back, with a bird at the back of the neck (see canvas placing diagrams)

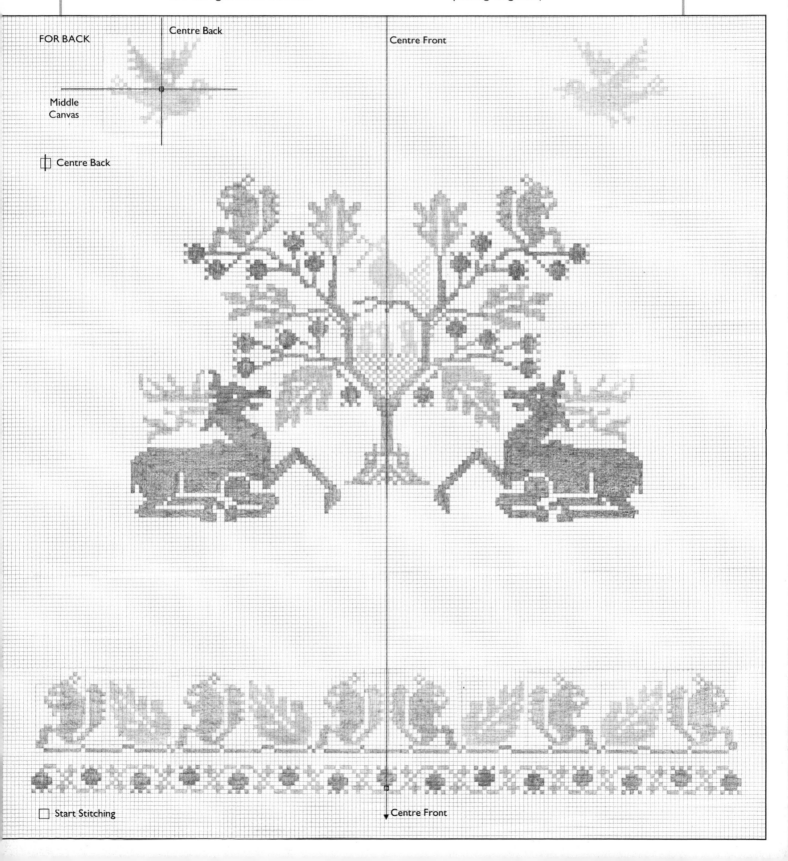

FOR BACK

Centre Back

Centre Front

Middle
Canvas

☐ Centre Back

☐ Start Stitching

↓ Centre Front

CANVAS GAUGE
8 holes per 2.5cm (1in)

QUANTITY
Three separate pieces:
56 x 61cm (22 x 24in)
56 x 12cm (22 x 5in)
12 x 12cm (5 x 5in)

STITCH SIZE
8 stitches per 2.5cm (1in)

EMBROIDERED AREA
Front: 53 x 56cm (21 x 22in)
Back band: 53 x 9cm (21 x 3½in)
Bird: 9 x 7.5cm (3½ x 3in)

1   Open the side seams of the garment from hem to underarm.
2   Following the Basic Instructions, tack in the CF and CB lines, and make relevant measurements.
3   Prepare and tape the canvas as Basic Instructions.
4   Position the canvas on the front of the garment as Fig 1 p101. Pin and tack. Make a grid of tacking stitches through both the canvas and garment, to prevent any slipping and distortion of the fabric (see Basic Instructions).
5   Position the two pieces of canvas for the back as Fig 2 p101. Pin and tack.
6   Start embroidering the front 2.5cm (1in) above the edge of the canvas at the point shown on the chart (see Fig 1). Work the lowest band first from CF to each side. Then continue as you please.
Note: Careful counting is necessary to ensure that the stags are positioned correctly.
7   For the band starting point on the back, work as for the front. For the decoration in the square at the neck, select a motif from the front chart. Count to find the centre stitch: then place the centre stitch on the centre of the canvas as Fig 2.
8   Finish as Basic Instructions.

FRUIT AND ANIMALS CHILD'S SWEATER

GARMENT
Child's sweater, round neck and T-shape sleeves

YARN
DMC Broder Medici (two strands of yarn in needle)

APPROXIMATE NUMBER OF SKEINS
8209 x 4   Blue
8417 x 1   Dark Green
8418 x 1   Pale Green
8419 x 2   Bright Green
8304 x 1   Gold
8168 x 1   Rust
8176 x 3   Orange
8166 x 1   Pale Orange

CANVAS GAUGE
10 holes per 2.5cm (1in)

QUANTITY
44 x 24cm (18½ x 10in)

CANVAS SIZE
42 x 20cm (16½ x 8in)

STITCH SIZE
10 stitches per 2.5cm (1in)

APPROXIMATE EMBROIDERED AREA
37 x 15cm (14½ x 6in)

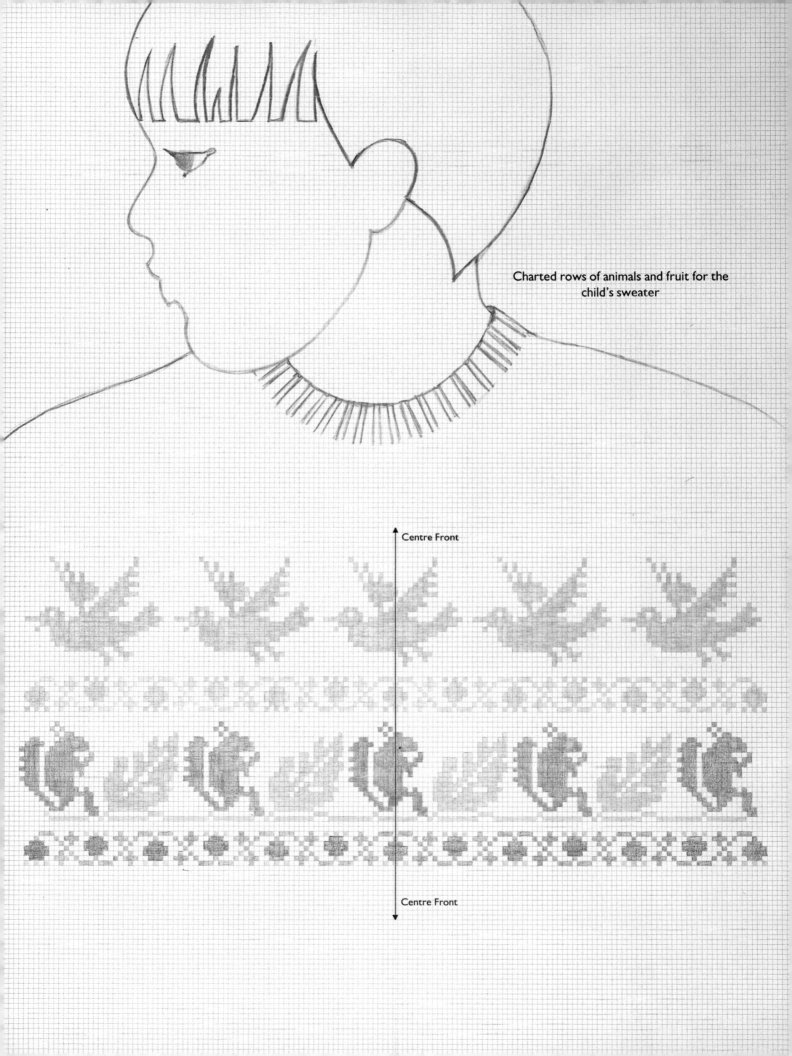

Charted rows of animals and fruit for the
child's sweater

Centre Front

Centre Front

Stags and leaves could be
embroidered on a
large-gauge canvas for a
man's knitted jacket

BERLIN WOOLWORK

◆

Early in the nineteenth century a German printer introduced coloured charted designs for canvas embroidery. Although silk and beads, and many different stitches and yarns were also used, the most popular stitch was cross or half-cross stitch, worked with Marino wool dyed in Berlin. At first the wools were naturally dyed in subtle shades, as they had been for centuries, but in the middle of the century chemical aniline dyes were invented, bringing much brighter, often garish, colours onto the market. Colours like magenta and mauve, and brilliant reds and greens were immensely popular; this whole area of embroidery was generally known as Berlin woolwork.

The range of colours from which the home embroiderer could choose was vast. For instance, from just one manufacturer, twenty-six different greens were each available in seven different tones, shading from very dark to ultra light. This wonderful palette of colours made it possible to blend tones in the most subtle way, almost like a painter, to create the three-dimensional appearance which is characteristic of Berlin work.

The fashion for Berlin work swept through Europe including Russia, eventually reaching America, New Zealand and Australia. The charted designs, along with the wools, were imported from Germany and France to England in their thousands during the first half of the century. The early hand-coloured charts were expensive, but later the invention of colour printing made mass production simple.

As always, flowers were a popular subject. Every variety of rose, together with carnations, pansies, violets and all the other blooms so beloved by Victorian gardeners were stitched into posies, swags, ropes and wreaths. Dogs were another favourite, especially Queen Victoria's spaniel, Dash, often depicted sitting on a cushion. Even famous paintings were copied in Berlin woolwork.

Many Berlin embroideries survive stitched onto heavy woollen grounds, and this was achieved in the same way as the embroideries are worked for this book – over canvas that is subsequently pulled away.

The industrious Victorians thought that 'to be idle is to be wicked', and in an age when a middle-class lady's life was desired and designed to be totally idle, needlework was the perfect pursuit to while away the hours. It is interesting to speculate that in the hectic world of the late twentieth century, this hugely popular Victorian fashion is perpetuated in the form of the traditional canvaswork pictures and cushions that we still enjoy embroidering today.

When the house was filled with cushions, firescreens, carpets and bell pulls, and one's husband clothed in waistcoat and smoking cap, with a receptacle in which to place his fob watch overnight, the Victorian embroideress had to find other outlets for her industry. Charitable bazaars were organised, selling pin cushions, caps and babies' bonnets, belts, braces, tea cosies and teapot stands – all decorated with specially scaled-down posies, butterflies, birds, playing cards, shells and even local heroes and heroines.

I find these small motifs particularly useful for decorating children's clothes, whilst I have repeated some of the favourite Victorian designs on modern knitwear, proving that good design can still look fresh and attractive today. The ability to imitate natural as well as man-made objects accurately, gives Berlin work its great vitality and variety. From the liveliest of the charts and existing embroideries, there is a wealth of motifs still waiting to be used.

PAISLEY SWEATER

The teardrop motif that we associate with the Paisley patterned shawls is an ancient Indian floral design thought to symbolise the Tree of Life. The original shawls were woven in Kashmir, and worn by men. Imported into England in the late eighteenth century, they were both costly and very fashionable. But they were soon imitated by Scottish weavers, notably in the town of Paisley. After Queen Victoria wore a shawl to the christening of her first-born son in 1842, the familiar motif became enormously popular. And soon the Paisley pattern featured in many canvaswork charts, particularly for slipper fronts or bags.

I have based this simple Paisley design on an original nineteenth-century canvaswork chart, and teamed it with a stylised floral border typical of those found on the shawls.

In strong single colours, the embroidery is worked onto a man's sweater. On a woman's cardigan and sweater, the multi-coloured design has a fringed edge suggesting an actual shawl.

◄ The teardrop Paisley motif comes from Kashmir, where it was used to decorate woven shawls which were worn by men

MAN'S SWEATER
GARMENT
Round-necked sweater with raglan or set-in T-shaped sleeves, in medium-weight knit

YARN
Anchor Tapestry Wool (Yarn)

NUMBER OF SKEINS
8612 x 3   Purple
8404 x 3   Burgundy
9540 x 4   Rust
8046 x 3   Ochre
8922 x 3   Green

CANVAS GAUGE
8 holes per 2.5cm (1in)

QUANTITY
Two pieces 53 x 36cm (21 x 14in)

STITCH SIZE
4 stitches per 2.5cm (1in)
(Embroider over every other hole)

EMBROIDERED AREA
Two pieces 48 x 30cm (19 x 12in)
(Whole design is repeated on the back)

1   Open the side seams of the garment from the hem to partway down the sleeve.
2   Tack in the CF and CB lines from hems to neck.
3   Prepare and mark the pieces of canvas.
4   Position the front canvas as Fig 1 p109. Pin and tack it into place.
5   Make a grid of tacking stitches across the canvas to hold it securely and prevent slipping.
6   Position and secure the back canvas in the same way (Fig 1).
7   Working over every other hole of the canvas, start stitching 2.5cm (1in) below the top edge of the canvas, at the point marked on the chart.
8   Finish as the Basic Instructions.

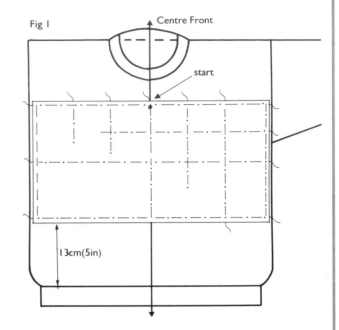

Fig 1

Centre Front

start

13cm(5in)

MULTI-COLOURED WOMAN'S SWEATER
GARMENT
Round-necked knitted sweater with T-shape set-in sleeves

YARN
Anchor Tapestry Wool (Yarn)

APPROXIMATE NUMBER OF SKEINS
8164 x 1   Orange
8968 x 1   Green
8204 x 1   Red
8822 x 1   Turquoise
8692 x 1   Blue
8366 x 1   Pink
9800 x 6   Black

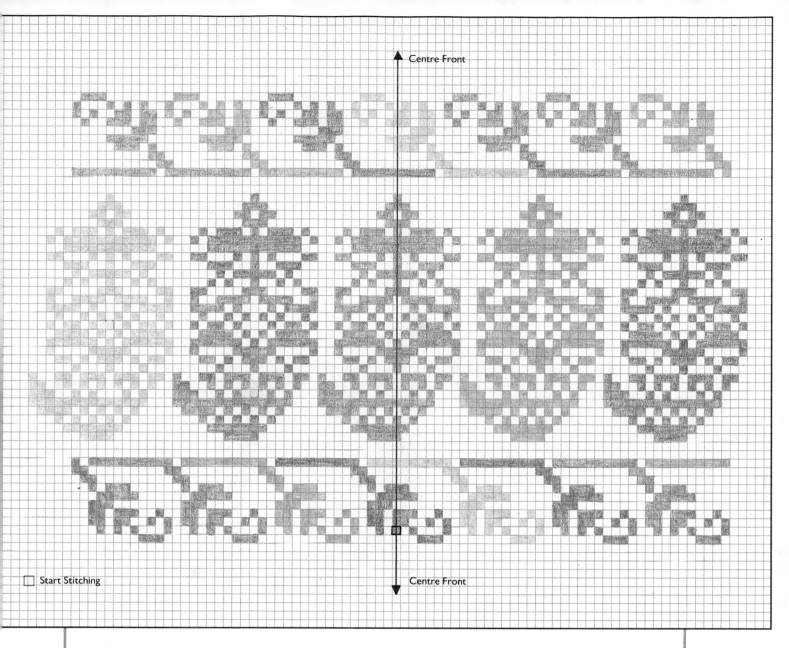

Centre Front

☐ Start Stitching

Centre Front

CANVAS GAUGE
12 holes per 2.5cm (1in)

QUANTITY
Approximately 53.5 x 38cm (21 x 15in)

STITCH SIZE
6 stitches per 2.5cm (1in)
(Embroider over every other hole)

APPROXIMATE EMBROIDERED AREA
Approximately 48 x 34.5cm (19 x 13½in)

▲ Chart for man's Paisley band. Repeat on the back of the garment (see canvas placing diagram), aligning bottom edges of front and back canvases

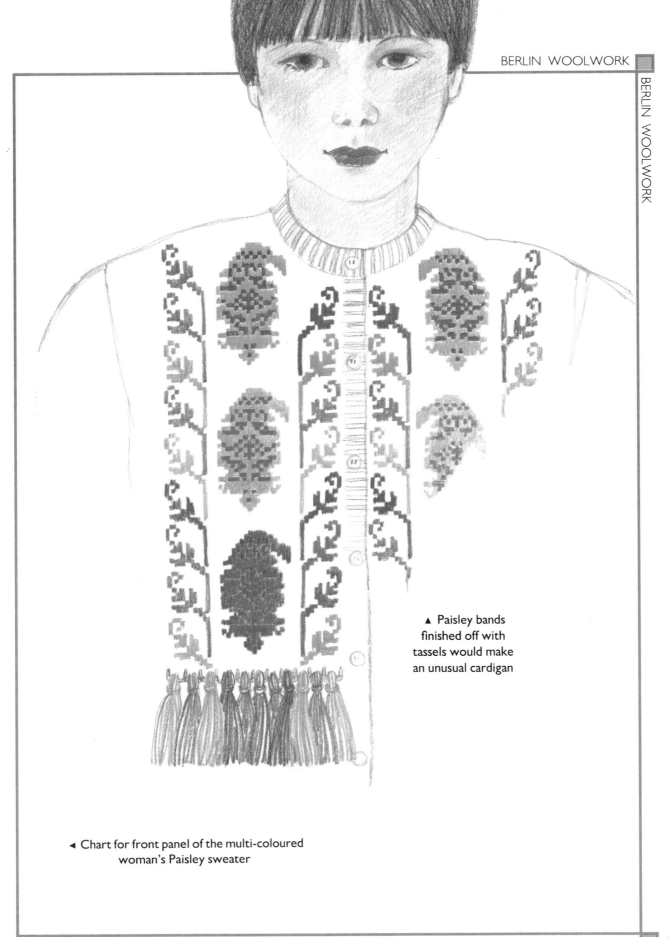

▲ Paisley bands
finished off with
tassels would make
an unusual cardigan

◀ Chart for front panel of the multi-coloured
woman's Paisley sweater

Continued across ►
the back of the
cardigan, the cross-
stitch interpretation
suggests metal and
glass beads in shades
of grey

This sophisticated ►
grisaille scrolls
design owes its
inspiration to the
intricate beadwork
that was fashionable
in the nineteenth
century

GRISAILLE SCROLLS CARDIGAN

Although Berlin woolwork was out of fashion by the 1870s, it continued to be stitched right up until the end of the century.

The chart on which I have based this design appeared in a 'Weldons' Sixpenny Series' devoted to cross stitch, probably published in the late 1920s/early 1930s. The design is certainly Victorian, and was to be embroidered on a 'black silk pochette in four shades of golden brown . . . the design is worked on fine canvas, the threads of which are afterwards drawn out'.

The four shades of grey wool used here simulate 'grisaille beadwork', the metal and glass bead decoration so popular in Victorian times. A simple banded version uses the original colours, suggesting brass or gold.

GARMENT
Round-neck button-through woman's cardigan, medium- to heavy-weight knit

YARN
Anchor Tapestry Wool (Yarn)

NUMBER OF SKEINS
9788 x 7   Silver
9790 x 4   Grey
9792 x 9   Dark Grey
9796 x 5   Charcoal

CANVAS GAUGE
14 holes per 2.5cm (1in)

QUANTITY
Front: two pieces 43 x 24cm (17 x 9½in)
Back: one piece 47 x 18cm (18½ x 7in)

STITCH SIZE
7 stitches per 2.5cm (1in)
(Embroider over every other hole)

EMBROIDERED AREA
Front: two pieces 38 x 19cm (15 x 7½in)
Back: 44.5 x 13cm (17½ x 5in)

Centre Back

Centre Back

Centre Design

Centre Design

Start Stitching

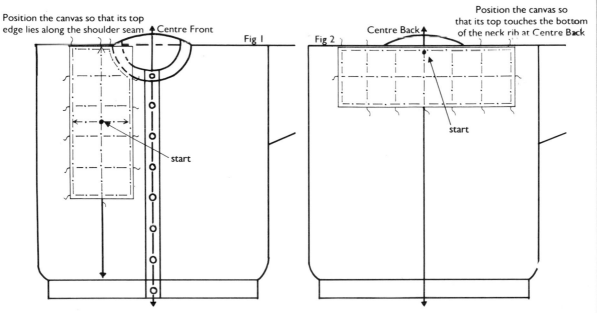

Position the canvas so that its top edge lies along the shoulder seam

Centre Front

Fig 1

start

Fig 2

Centre Back

Position the canvas so that its top touches the bottom of the neck rib at Centre Back

start

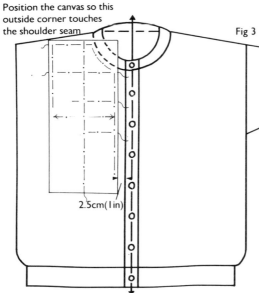

Position the canvas so this outside corner touches the shoulder seam

Fig 3

2.5cm(1in)

◄ Chart for fronts and back yoke of grisaille scrolls cardigan

I On both sides of the front, measure 2.5cm (1in) along the shoulder seam from the neck rib.

2 Tack a vertical line down the garment from this point to the bottom ribbing.

3 Make sure this line is straight by checking the measurement from the CF button-band to the line, at points all down the front.

4 Prepare and mark the two front pieces of canvas.

5 Fold them in half lengthways and mark the centre line.

6 Position the front pieces of canvas as in Fig 1, matching the lengthways centre line of the canvas to the tacked line on the garment.

7 Pin and tack them into place.

8 Make a grid of tacking stitches across the canvas to secure it firmly and prevent slipping.

9 On the back, measure and mark the CB line.

10 Prepare and mark back canvas.

11 Position the canvas as Fig 2.

12 Pin and tack into place.

13 Make a grid of tacking stitches across the canvas, as before.

Note: If your garment has a slanting shoulder seam, position the pieces of canvas as Fig 3.

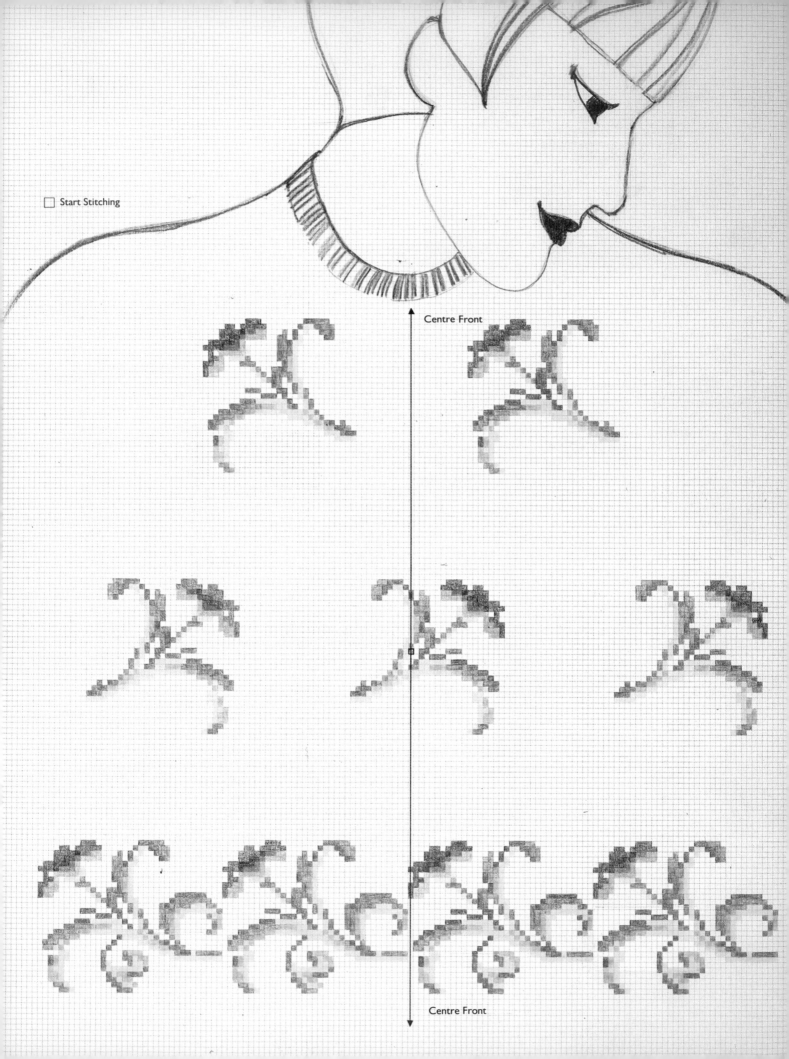

Start Stitching

Centre Front

Centre Front

14 Working over every other hole of the canvas, start stitching the front at the centre points as marked on the chart.

15 Start stitching the back at the point marked on the chart, 2.5cm (1in) below the top of the canvas.

16 Finish as the Basic Instructions.

GRISAILLE SCROLLS SWEATER
GARMENT
Round-neck woman's sweater, medium-weight knit

YARN
Anchor Tapestry Wool (Yarn)

APPROXIMATE NUMBER OF SKEINS
8490 x 1	Magenta
8488 x 1	Bright Pink
8486 x 1	Pink
8484 x 1	Pale Pink
9264 x 3	Olive Green
9202 x 3	Mid Green
9200 x 1	Lime Green
9196 x 3	Light Green

CANVAS GAUGE
8 holes per 2.5cm (1in)

QUANTITY
Approximately 43 x 48cm (17 x 19in)

STITCH SIZE
8 stitches per 2.5cm (1in)

APPROXIMATE EMBROIDERED AREA
Approximately 38 x 43cm (15 x 17in), including one flower at back neck

◄ Charted coloured sprigs for the grisaille scrolls sweater. Place a single sprig at the back of the neck

◄ The original back yoke grisaille scrolls design could be used in a gold colour range, for a yoke completed by a buttonhole-stitched and fringed border

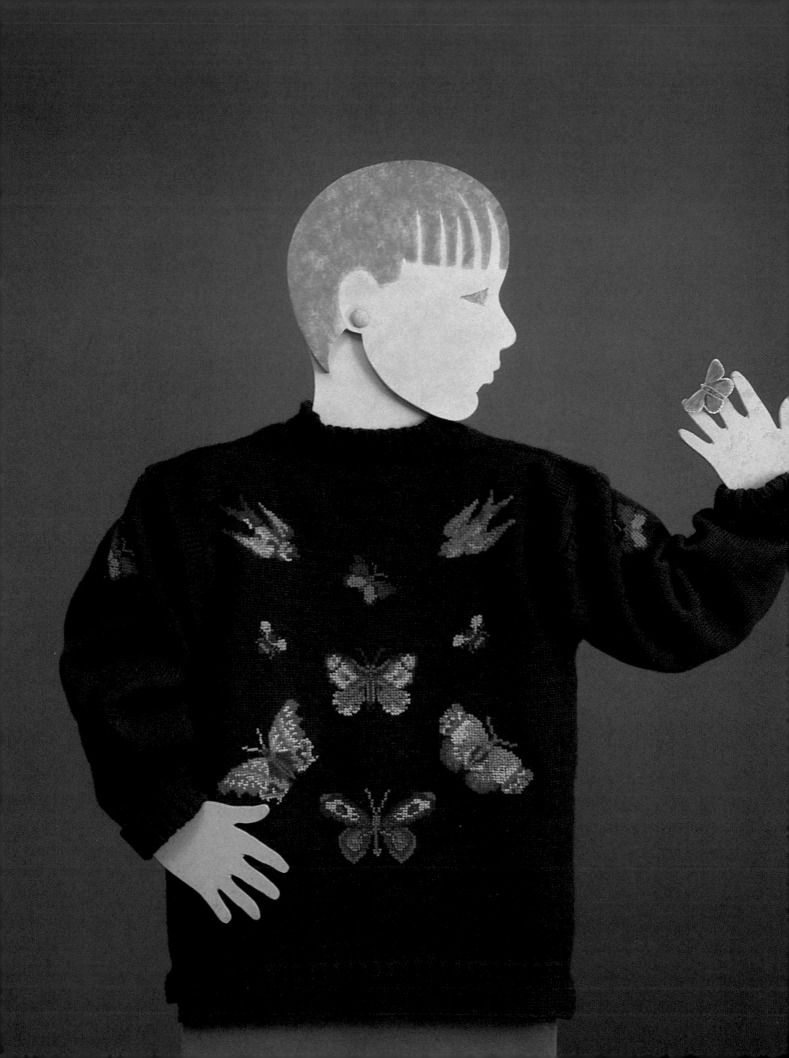

BUTTERFLIES, BIRDS AND BEES SWEATER

The Victorians, stimulated by new scientific discoveries, loved to collect and preserve natural things: they were fascinated by shells, birds' eggs, fossils and butterflies. These interests are reflected in their embroidery. All manner of creatures are depicted in Berlin woolwork, from farmyard animals through exotic species to family pets and assorted insects.

The butterfly was a particularly popular motif, its varied strong patterns often appearing as part of a bigger scene, or fitted into corners on small patchwork pieces. These butterflies were on a patchwork Berlin-embroidered settee in the Welsh Folk Museum, which was also the inspiration for other designs in the book. I found the two birds on totally different embroideries, one French, one English, in different colours; but both had obviously been worked from the same chart.

Set as spot motifs on a child's jumper, all the flying creatures make a brilliant display. I decided to use the original colours on the patchwork design, and rows of bees, birds and butterflies are effective as simple repeating bands.

CHILD'S SWEATER
GARMENT
Child's round-neck sweater, T-shape sleeves, (or V-neck sweater with the design lowered by about 5cm (2in))

YARN
DMC Laine Tapisserie
(work with two lengths of yarn in the needle)

NUMBERS OF SKEINS
8129 x 1   Peach
8128 x 1   Brick Pink
8102 x 1   Red
8326 x 1   Yellow
8302 x 1   Ochre
8323 x 1   Dark Ochre
8114 x 1   Brown

8997 x 1   Pale Turquoise
8996 x 1   Mid Turquoise
8995 x 1   Dark Turquoise
8794 x 1   Purple
8720 x 1   Pale Blue
8899 x 1   Mid Blue
8799 x 1   Dark Blue

CANVAS GAUGE
10 holes per 2.5cm (1in)

QUANTITY
Front: 34.5 x 40.5cm (13½ x 16in)
Back: 6.5 x 6.5cm (2½ x 2½in)
Sleeves: Two pieces 10 x 10cm (4 x 4in)

STITCH SIZE
10 stitches per 2.5cm (1in)

EMBROIDERED AREA
29 x 36cm (11½ x 14in)

◄ This collection of flying creatures recalls the Victorian interest in nature

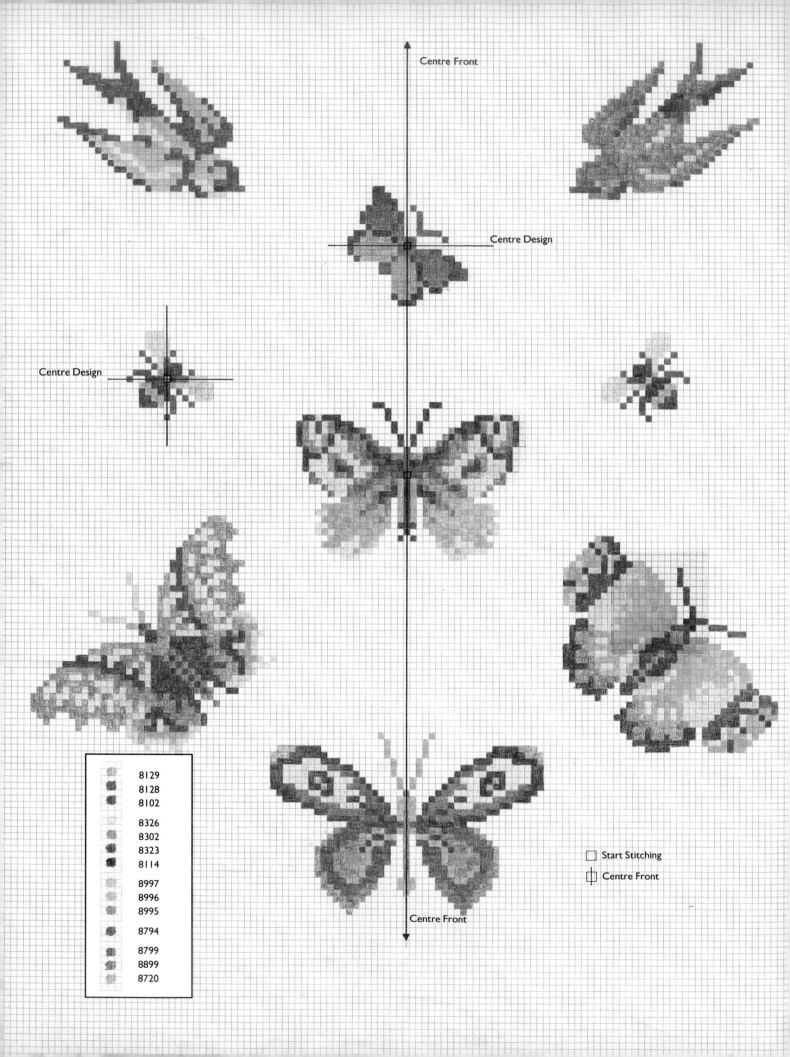

Centre Front

Centre Design

Centre Design

8129
8128
8102

8326
8302
8323
8114

8997
8996
8995

8794

8799
8899
8720

Start Stitching

Centre Front

Centre Front

Rows of flying creatures would be ideal for a child's sweater

◄ Chart for child's butterflies, birds and bees sweater. The small blue butterfly is repeated at the top of the sleeves, and a bee is placed at the back of the neck (see canvas placing diagram)

1 Open the side seams of the sweater from the hem to armholes.

2 Tack in the CF, CB and CS lines.

3 Prepare and mark canvas pieces.

4 Fold each canvas lengthways and mark to establish the centre point.

5 Position the front canvas as Fig 1 (overleaf). Pin and tack into place.

6 Make a grid of tacking stitches over the canvas to hold it securely and prevent slipping.

7 Position the back canvas as Fig 2 (overleaf). Pin and tack into place.

8 Position each sleeve canvas as Fig 3 (overleaf). Pin and tack into place.

9 On all the canvases, start the embroidery with the stitch shown on the chart. Work with two lengths of yarn in the needle.

10 Finish as the Basic Instructions.

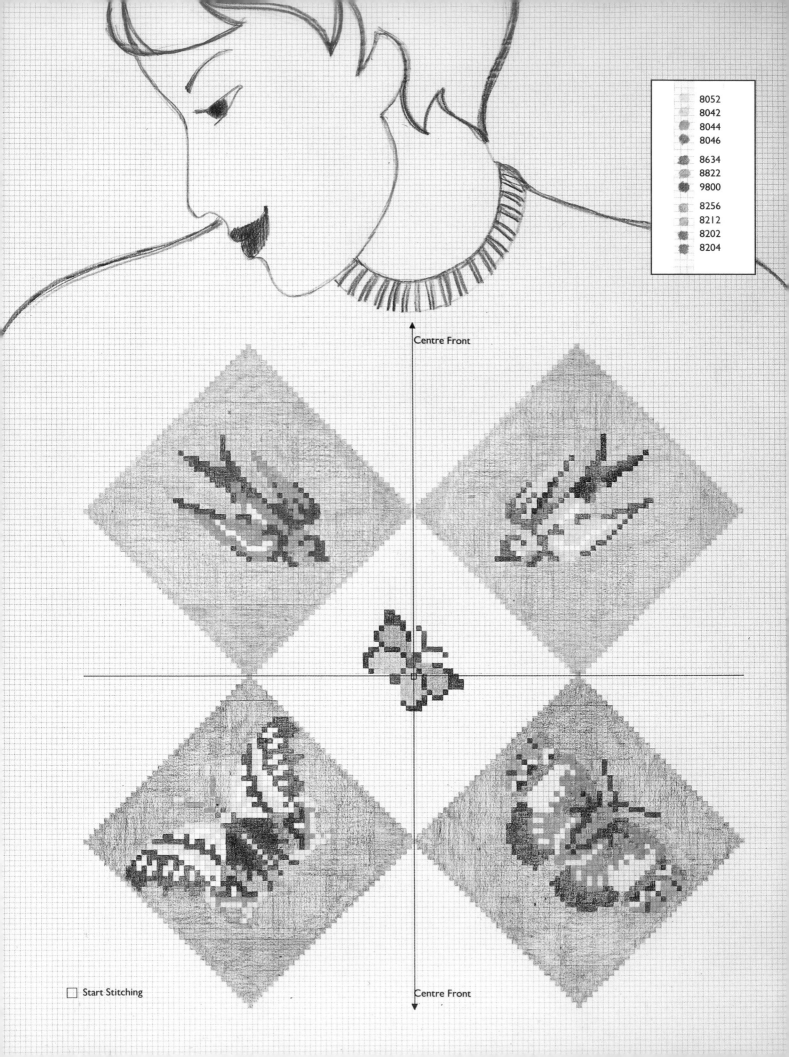

Centre Front

	8052
	8042
	8044
	8046
	8634
	8822
	9800
	8256
	8212
	8202
	8204

☐ Start Stitching

Centre Front

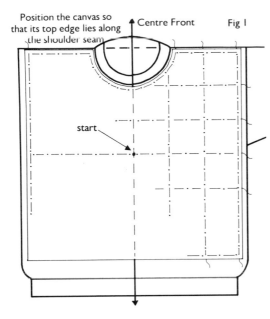

Position the canvas so that its top edge lies along the shoulder seam

Centre Front

Fig I

start

ADULT'S SWEATER

GARMENT
Round- or V-neck adult's sweater, with raglan or set-in sleeves

YARN
Anchor Tapestry Yarn

APPROXIMATE NUMBER OF SKEINS
8052 x 1	Cream
8042 x 1	Yellow
8044 x 1	Ochre
8046 x 1	Dark Ochre
8634 x 6	Blue
8822 x 6	Turquoise
9800 x 1	Black
8256 x 1	Pale Pink
8212 x 1	Peach
8202 x 1	Brick Pink
8204 x 1	Red

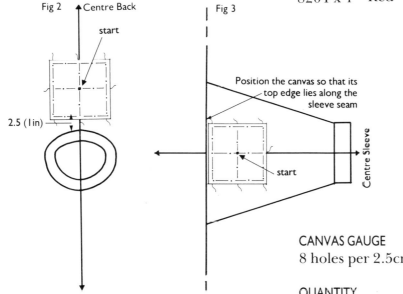

Fig 2

Centre Back

start

2.5 (1in)

Fig 3

Position the canvas so that its top edge lies along the sleeve seam

Centre Sleeve

start

CANVAS GAUGE
8 holes per 2.5cm (1in)

QUANTITY
Approximately 46 x 46cm (18 x 18in)

STITCH SIZE
8 stitches per 2.5cm (1in)

APPROXIMATE EMBROIDERED AREA
Approximately 41 x 41cm (16 x 16in)

◄ Charted patchwork butterfly adult's sweater, worked in the original Victorian colours

SHADED INTERLACE SWEATER

By following in the footsteps of the Victorian needleworkers, and re-colouring these earlier designs using graded tones of colour, one can fully appreciate the fascination of Berlin woolwork. Samplers of the fashionable needlework were made by professional needlewomen, worked on long narrow strips of canvas, to be rolled up and kept in a workbox. Many are still in existence, measuring anything up to around five metres (16ft) in length. All types of patterns are to be found on them, but time and again the same interlocking designs are seen transformed by the light and shaded colours of Berlin wools.

Strong colours are used to great effect, and for this mid-grey sweater I have used a much larger size of stitch, in keeping with the bold designs favoured by the later Victorians. The design in the photograph relies on the tones of wool for its effect. The other designs are in-filled like jewelled bands, or the repeated tile patterns so often found on later samplers.

MAN'S SWEATER

GARMENT
Round-neck man's sweater with raglan or T-shape set-in sleeves, medium-gauge knit

YARN
Anchor Tapestry Wool (Yarn)

NUMBER OF SKEINS

8040 x 4	Pale Yellow
8042 x 4	Yellow
8044 x 4	Ochre
8046 x 4	Brown
8918 x 4	Pale Green
8926 x 4	Green
8924 x 4	Dark Green
8904 x 4	Bottle Green

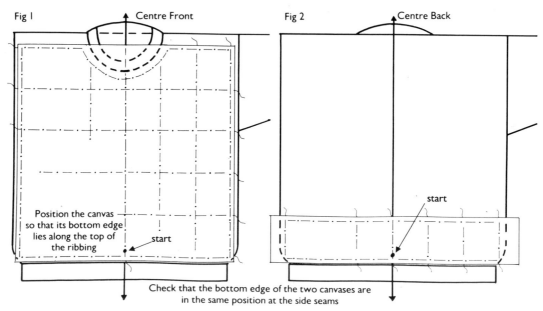

Fig 1 — Centre Front

Position the canvas so that its bottom edge lies along the top of the ribbing — start

Fig 2 — Centre Back

start

Check that the bottom edge of the two canvases are in the same position at the side seams

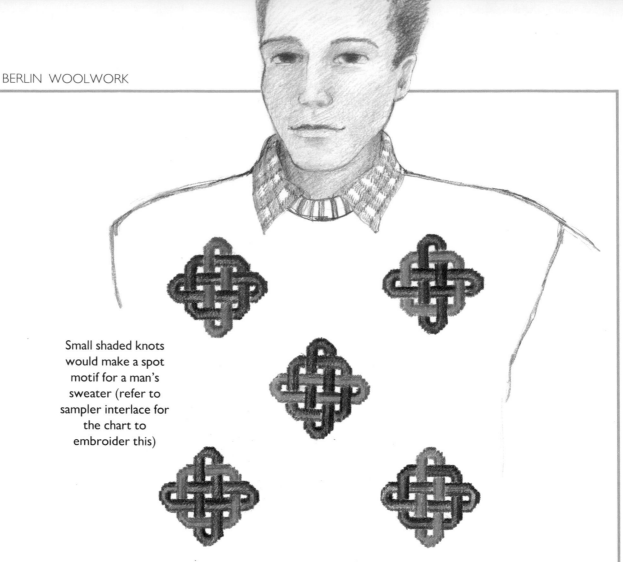

Small shaded knots would make a spot motif for a man's sweater (refer to sampler interlace for the chart to embroider this)

CANVAS GAUGE
10 holes per 2.5cm (1in)

QUANTITY
Front: 56 x 51cm (22 x 20in)
Back: 50 x 18cm (20 x 7in)

STITCH SIZE
5 stitches per 2.5cm (1in)
(Embroider over every other hole)

EMBROIDERED AREA
Front: 51 x 46cm (20 x 18in)
Back: 44.5 x 13cm (17½ x 5in)

1 Open the side seams of the garment from the hem to partway down the sleeve.
2 Tack in the CF and CB lines.

3 Prepare the two pieces of canvas, marking the CF and CB lines.
4 Fold in half lengthways to find the centre point of the larger canvas.
5 Position the front canvas as Fig 1 p126. Pin and tack into place.
6 Position the back canvas as Fig 2 p126. Pin and tack into place.
7 Make a grid of tacking stitches across both pieces of canvas, to hold them securely and prevent slipping.
8 Working over every other hole of the canvas, start embroidering at the positions marked on the charts, beginning with the lower band on the front. Then go to the lower edge of the knot.
9 Finish as the Basic Instructions.

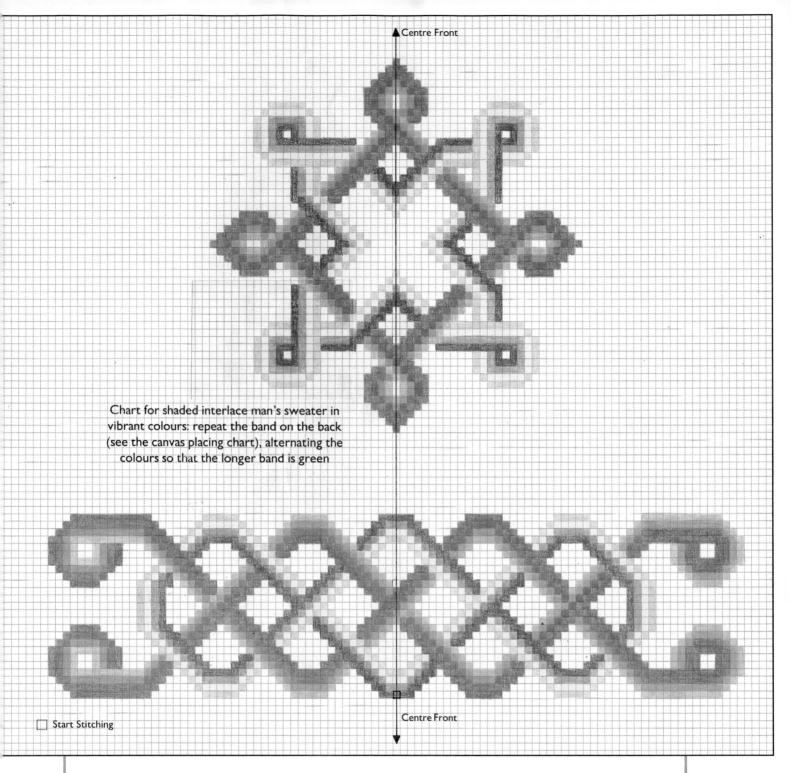

Chart for shaded interlace man's sweater in vibrant colours: repeat the band on the back (see the canvas placing chart), alternating the colours so that the longer band is green

□ Start Stitching

Centre Front

WOMAN'S SWEATER

GARMENT
Round-neck woman's sweater, set-in
T-shape sleeves, medium-weight knit

YARN
Anchor Tapestry Wool (Yarn)

APPROXIMATE NUMBER OF SKEINS
9796 x 2   Dark Grey
9792 x 4   Mid Grey
9788 x 2   Light Grey

CANVAS GAUGE
12 holes per 2.5cm (1in)

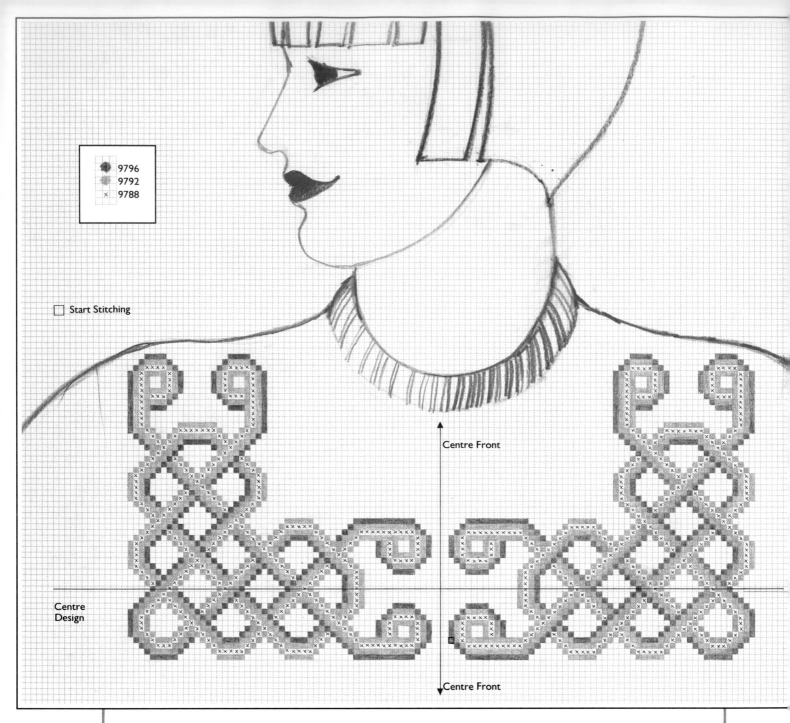

9796
9792
9788

Start Stitching

Centre Front

Centre Front

Centre
Design

CANVAS SIZE
48 x 27cm (19 x 10½in)

STITCH SIZE
6 stitches per 2.5cm (1in)
(Embroider over every other hole)

APPROXIMATE EMBROIDERED AREA
Approximately 43 x 21.5cm (17 x 8½in)

Chart showing one-colour square yoke for the shaded interlace woman's sweater

Note: The design is very effective when worked on the back as well. Use the same size piece of canvas as for the front, and position it with its top edge lying along the neck rib, matching up the CB lines. Use double the quantities of yarn stated above.

TROMPE L'ŒIL SWEATER

The literal meaning of *trompe l'œil* is 'to deceive the eye'. The subtle variations of light and shade that could be achieved with the enormous range of colour tones available in the Berlin wools, enabled flat embroidery to appear three dimensional.

Bands of pattern finished with trompe l'œil tassels could be used on a woman's cardigan

Various other textiles were copied: plaits and cords look as if they are actually twisted together, ribbons fold and tie themselves into bows, rows of tassels appear to be hanging from braids. Tartans and plaids, as well as Florentine tapestry, were copied.

The main design for this sweater is a simple yoke of tartan ribbon with twisted braids and tassels. I've also charted a banded design of ribbons, plaits and braids, giving you the opportunity to experiment with more involved deceptions.

The illusion is created by very dense embroidery, so wait until you have enough experience to tackle this type of design, as both the stitching itself, and the subsequent removal of the threads, are fairly labour-intensive.

GARMENT
Round-neck sweater with T-shape set-in or raglan sleeves; medium to heavy knit; fairly close-knitted fabric, as the embroidery is very dense

YARN
Anchor Tapestry Wool (Yarn)

NUMBER OF SKEINS
8042 x 1	Pale Yellow
8044 x 9	Mid Yellow
8046 x 3	Ochre
8048 x 2	Brown
8366 x 1	Pale Pink
8400 x 2	Mid Pink
8404 x 7	Dark Pink
8426 x 2	Burgundy
8634 x 3	Blue
9008 x 3	Green

CANVAS GAUGE
14 holes per 2.5cm (1in)

QUANTITY
50 x 55cm (20 x 22in)

STITCH SIZE
7 stitches per 2.5cm (1in)
(Embroider over every other hole)

EMBROIDERED AREA
45 x 50cm (18 x 20in)

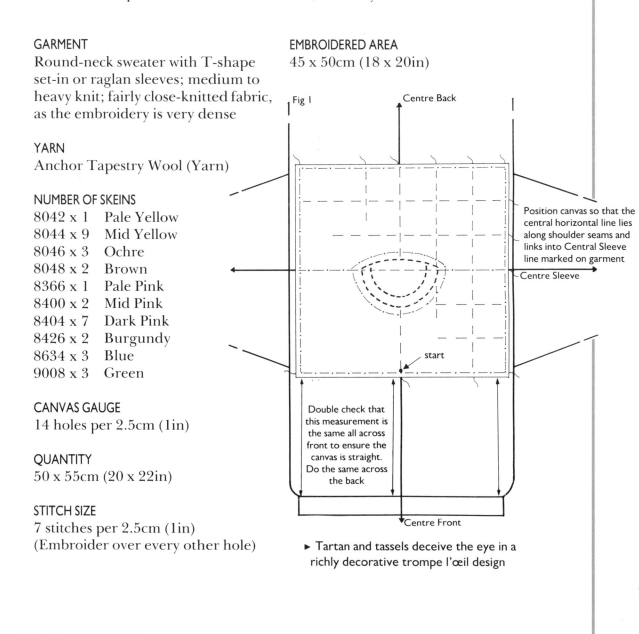

Fig 1

Centre Back

Position canvas so that the central horizontal line lies along shoulder seams and links into Central Sleeve line marked on garment

Centre Sleeve

start

Double check that this measurement is the same all across front to ensure the canvas is straight. Do the same across the back

Centre Front

▶ Tartan and tassels deceive the eye in a richly decorative trompe l'œil design

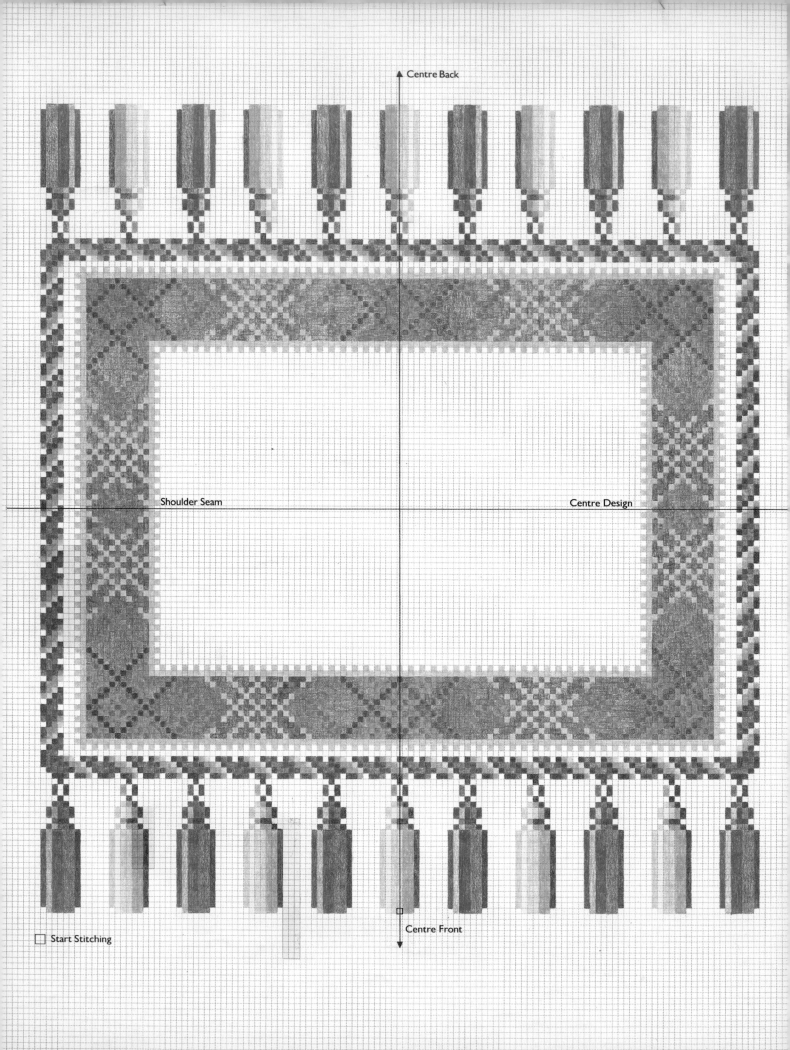

Centre Back

Shoulder Seam

Centre Design

Centre Front

Start Stitching

1 Open the side seams of the garment from hem to cuffs.
2 Lay the garment out flat.
3 Tack in the CF, CB and CS lines.
4 Prepare and mark the canvas.
5 Fold in half lengthways and mark this line as well.
6 Position the canvas on the garment as Fig 1.
7 Pin and tack into place.
8 Double check that the canvas is straight, by measuring from the bottom of the canvas to the bottom ribs on the garment, at several points: it is important to ensure that the strong horizontal straight line of the tartan strip will be level, in order to avoid any sense of distortion.
9 Make a grid of tacking stitches across the canvas to secure it firmly and prevent slipping.
10 Working on the wrong side, tack the canvas to the garment around the neck rib.
11 Working over every other hole of the canvas, start stitching on the front of the garment at the point marked on the chart, 2.5cm (1in) up from the bottom of the canvas.
12 Finish as the Basic Instructions.
Note: The dense embroidery needs to be very wet (soaked), to enable the threads of canvas to be removed easily.

BANDED TROMPE L'ŒIL SWEATER
GARMENT
Round-neck woollen sweater, medium to dense knit. (Design would also work well in cottons on a sweatshirt)

YARN
Anchor Tapestry Wool (Yarn)

APPROXIMATE NUMBER OF SKEINS
8042 x 2 Dark Yellow
8938 x 1 Dark Turquoise
8920 x 1 Mid Turquoise
8918 x 1 Pale Turquoise
8414 x 2 Very Pale Turquoise
8630 x 1 Dark Blue
8628 x 1 Mid Blue
8626 x 1 Pale Blue
8624 x 1 Very Pale Blue
8310 x 1 Dark Pink
8308 x 1 Mid Pink
8304 x 2 Pale Pink
8302 x 1 Very Pale Pink

CANVAS GAUGE
10 holes per 2.5cm (1in)

QUANTITY
52.5 x 46cm (21 x 18in)

STITCH SIZE
5 stitches per 2.5cm (1in)
(Worked over every other hole of canvas)

APPROXIMATE EMBROIDERED AREA
48 x 40.5cm (19 x 16in)

► Square yoke chart for the trompe l'œil sweater, showing front and back

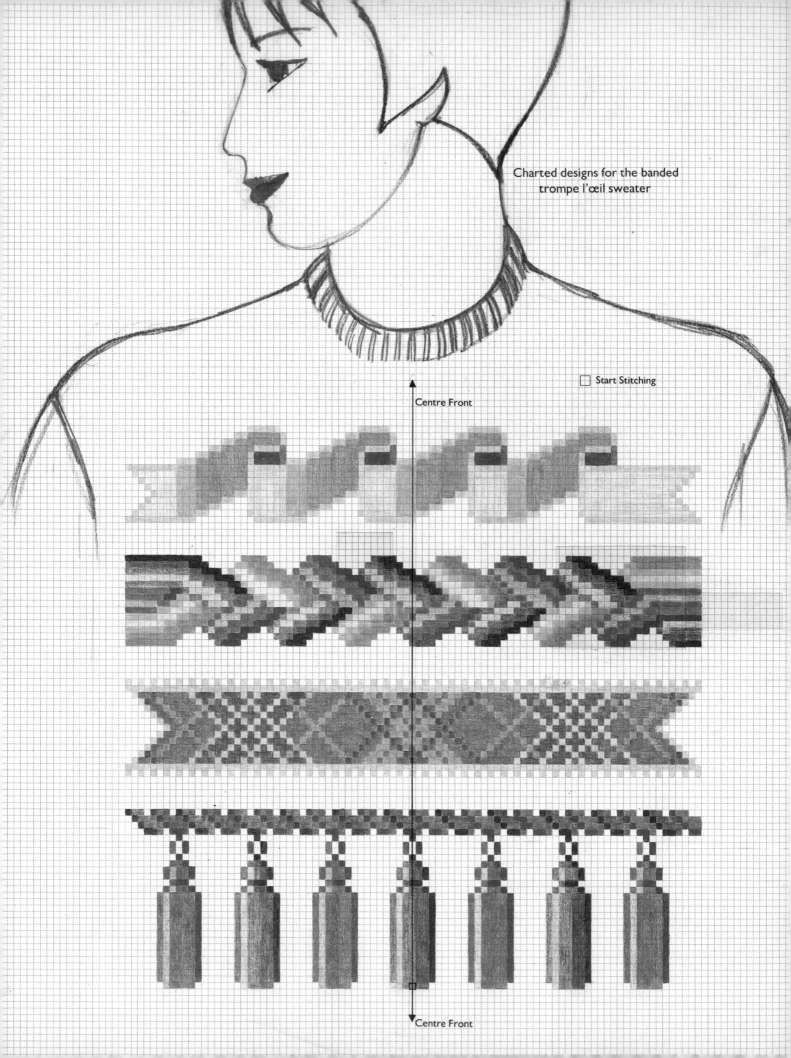

Charted designs for the banded
trompe l'œil sweater

☐ Start Stitching

Centre Front

Centre Front

ROSES AND VIOLETS GARLANDED SWEATER

In the nineteenth century new plant varieties from the expanding British Empire were collected and bred with native varieties. Yellow China roses crossed with home-grown white, pink and red roses, gave a wider variety of colours and shapes, and violet enthusiasts developed the fuller-faced pansies that we know and love today.

I have created a garland of pink and violet flowers tied around the neck of a sweater with a large blue bow. A band of yellow roses bordered by twisted ribbons is charted, whilst the temptation to use the bow alone, simply tied around the neck, proved irresistible.

GARMENT
Round-neck, long- or short-sleeved sweater with either T-shape set-in or raglan sleeves. The embroidery may cover part of the sleeve head as well as front and back of bodice

YARN
Anchor Tapestry Wool (Yarn)

NUMBER OF SKEINS
8362 x 2   Palest Pink
8366 x 2   Pale Pink
8368 x 2   Mid Pink
8400 x 2   Dark Pink
8352 x 2   Dark Red
8546 x 2   Pale Mauve
8548 x 2   Mauve
8552 x 2   Purple
9164 x 2   Pale Green
9168 x 2   Mid Green
9202 x 2   Dark Green
8604 x 1   Pale Blue
8608 x 1   Dark Blue
8024 x 1   Gold

CANVAS GAUGE
10 holes per 2.5cm (1in)

QUANTITY
56 x 61cm (22 x 24in)

STITCH SIZE
5 stitches per 2.5cm (1in)
(Embroider over every other hole)

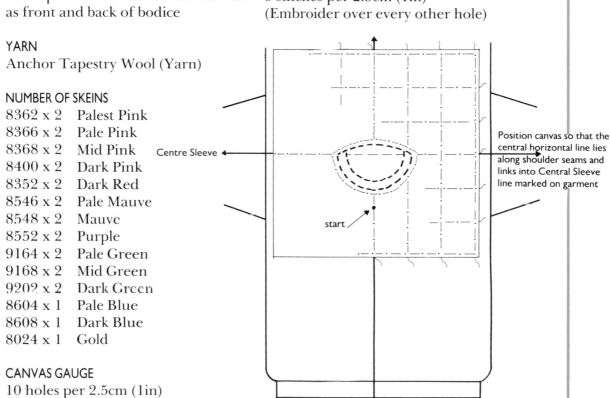

Centre Sleeve

Position canvas so that the central horizontal line lies along shoulder seams and links into Central Sleeve line marked on garment

start

Centre Front

An extravagant ▶ bow of embroidered ribbon ties the garland behind the neck

◀ Roses and violets were Victorian favourites, and they combine beautifully on this very feminine sweater

EMBROIDERED AREA
48 x 51cm (19 x 20in)

1 Open the sweater along the side seams and down the sleeve seams.
2 Lay the garment out flat.
3 Mark the CF, CB and CS lines.
4 Prepare and mark the canvas.
5 Fold the canvas in half lengthways and mark this line as well.
6 Position the canvas on the garment as Fig 1.
7 Pin and tack into place.
8 Make a grid of tacking stitches across the canvas to secure it firmly and prevent slipping.
9 Working on the wrong side, firmly tack the canvas to the garment around the neck rib.
10 Working over every other hole of the canvas, start to embroider at the point marked on the chart.
11 Finish as the Basic Instructions.

ROSES AND RIBBONS SWEATSHIRT
GARMENT
Woman's round-neck sweatshirt with T-shape set-in sleeves

YARN
Anchor Stranded Cottons (floss)
(Use all six strands: separate individual strands, then place together before threading needle)

APPROXIMATE NUMBER OF SKEINS
300 x 1	Cream
301 x 2	Pale Yellow
302 x 1	Mid Yellow
303 x 1	Dark Yellow
803 x 1	Ochre
203 x 1	Pale Green
204 x 1	Mid Green
205 x 1	Dark Green
342 x 1	Palest Purple
108 x 1	Pale Purple
110 x 2	Mid Purple
112 x 1	Dark Purple

CANVAS GAUGE
8 holes per 2.5cm (1in)

QUANTITY
Approximately 36 x 20cm (14 x 8in)

STITCH SIZE
8 stitches per 2.5cm (1in)

APPROXIMATE EMBROIDERED AREA
30.5 x 15cm (12 x 6in)

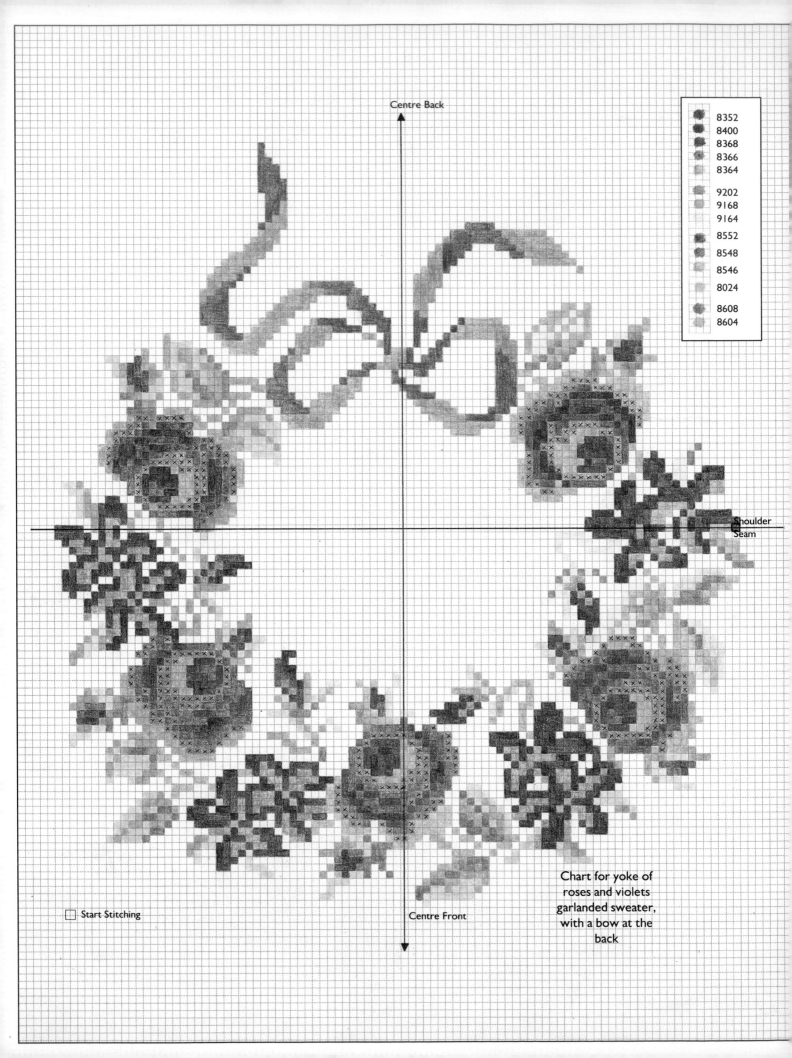

Centre Back

Shoulder Seam

▩	8352
▩	8400
▩	8368
▩	8366
▩	8364
▩	9202
▩	9168
▩	9164
▩	8552
▩	8548
▩	8546
▩	8024
▩	8608
▩	8604

☐ Start Stitching

Centre Front

Chart for yoke of roses and violets garlanded sweater, with a bow at the back

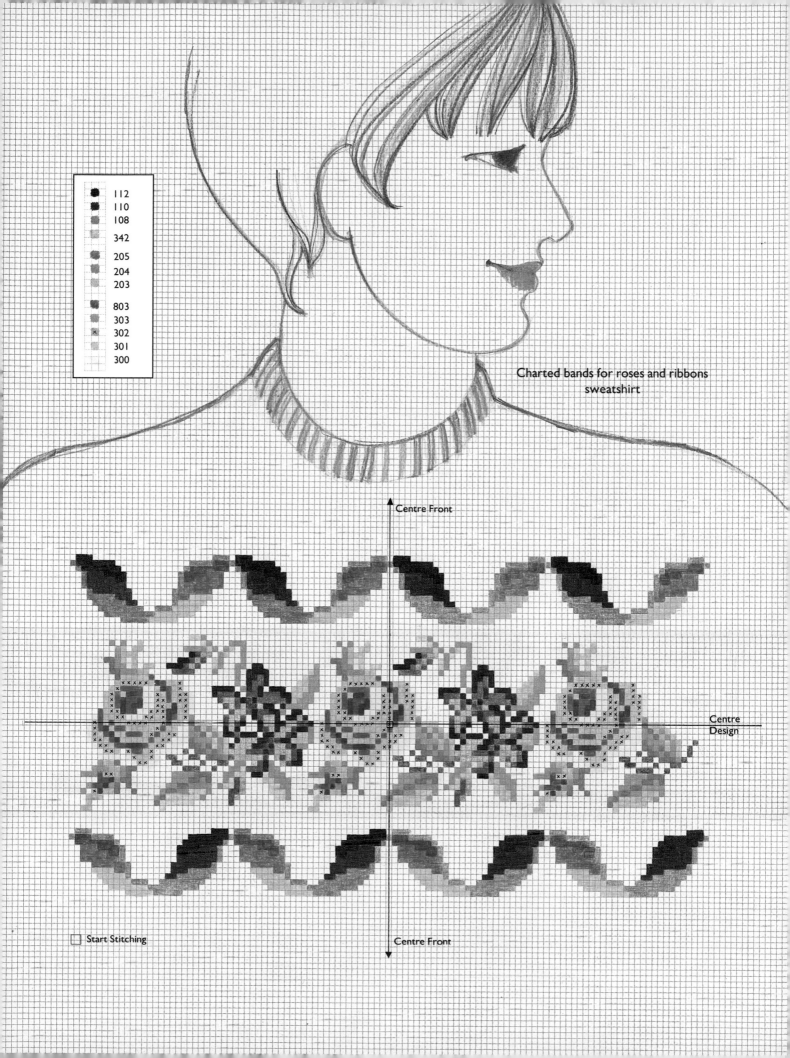

●	112
	110
	108
	342
	205
	204
	203
	803
	303
×	302
	301
	300

Charted bands for roses and ribbons sweatshirt

Centre Front

Centre Design

Centre Front

☐ Start Stitching

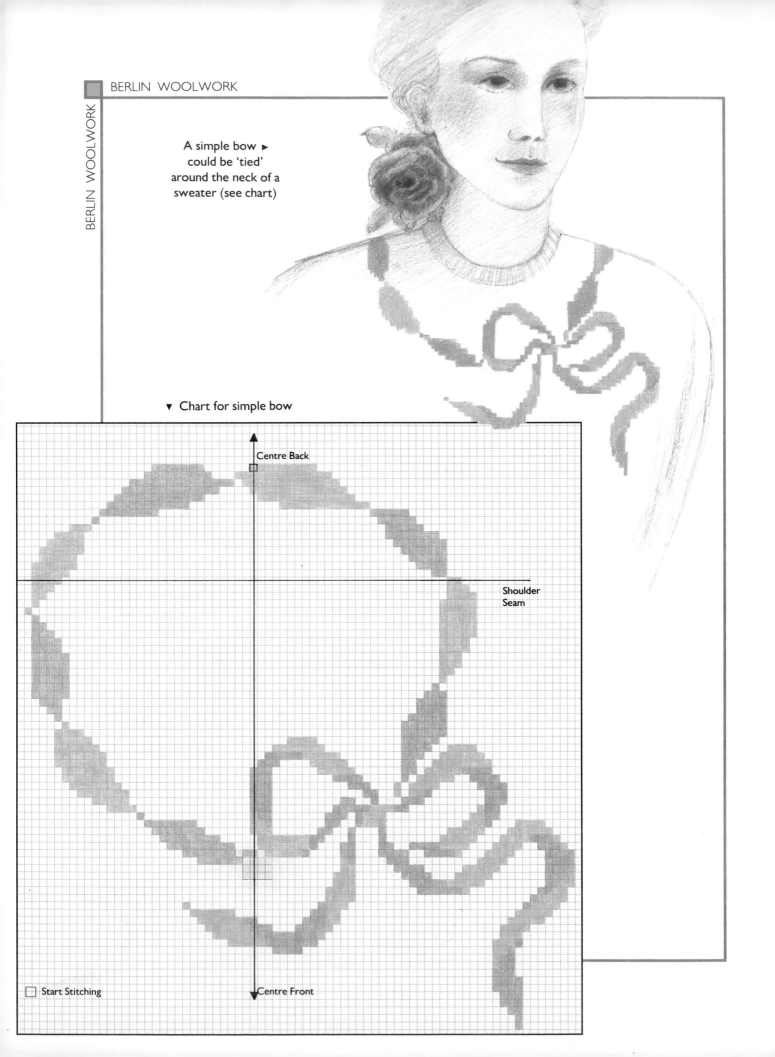

A simple bow ▶
could be 'tied'
around the neck of a
sweater (see chart)

▼ Chart for simple bow

Centre Back

Shoulder
Seam

Start Stitching   Centre Front

SHELLS AND SEAWEED SWEATER

Berlin wool was used by sailors in their long off-duty hours at sea, to create accurate representations of the ships on which they sailed. But these strong individual embroideries are made up of long straight stitches, and so are not charted for cross stitch.

Having searched vainly for small motifs with a naval connection, I turned to the sea for a theme – and found shells. Softly shaded and subtly coloured, they were depicted on a patchwork settee in the Welsh Folk Museum. The swaying seaweed (taken from a sampler) adds movement to a fashionably new, but evocatively Victorian, design.

A very large version of the shells in stronger colours is charted to cover the front of a sweater. The patchwork effect has been created to recall the original source of inspiration.

This design is not difficult, but concentration is needed to work the subtle colour scheme, so don't try it until you are practised in following the charts.

GARMENT
Round-neck woman's sweater with T-shape set-in or raglan sleeves, medium-weight knit

YARN
Anchor Tapestry Wool (Yarn)

NUMBER OF SKEINS
8040 x 1	Pale Yellow
8042 x 1	Mid Yellow
8044 x 2	Dark Yellow
8046 x 1	Ochre
9306 x 2	Pale Green
9202 x 1	Mid Green
9264 x 1	Dark Green
9508 x 2	Pale Peach
9510 x 1	Peach
9600 x 1	Dark Peach
9640 x 2	Brown
8330 x 1	Dark Terracotta
9620 x 2	Pink
8510 x 3	Deep Pink
8512 x 1	Plum
8546 x 1	Mauve
8548 x 1	Dark Mauve

CANVAS GAUGE
10 holes per 2.5cm (1in)

QUANTITY
Front: 51 x 42cm (20 x 16½in)
Back: 13 x 13cm (5 x 5in)

STITCH SIZE
5 stitches per 2.5cm (1in)
(Embroider over every other hole)

EMBROIDERED AREA
Front: 46 x 37cm (18 x 14½in)
Back: 10 x 10cm (4 x 4in)

I Open the side seams of the garment, and partway down the sleeves.
2 Lay the garment out flat and mark the CF and CB lines.
3 Prepare and mark the pieces of canvas.
4 Position the front canvas as Fig 1. Pin and tack into place.
5 Make a grid of tacking stitches across the canvas to hold it securely and prevent slipping.

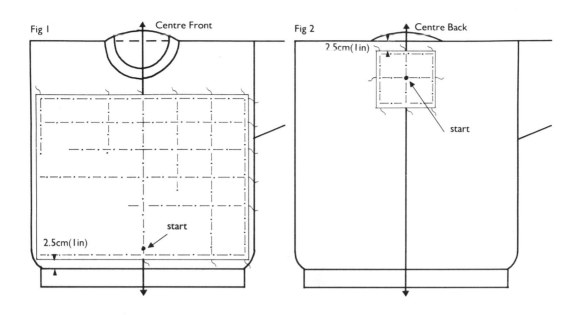

6 Position the back canvas as Fig 2. Pin and tack into place.

7 Make a grid of tacking stitches across the canvas as for the front.

8 Working over every other hole of the canvas, begin the embroidery at the point marked on the chart, 2.5cm (1in) above the bottom edge of the canvas.

9 Finish as the Basic Instructions.

SHELL SWEATSHIRT

GARMENT
Round-neck sweatshirt

YARN
Anchor Stranded Cotton (floss)
(Use all six strands: separate the individual strands, then place them together again before threading the needle)

APPROXIMATE NUMBER OF SKEINS
886 x 1   Pale Yellow
874 x 1   Mid Yellow
907 x 2   Dark Yellow
277 x 1   Ochre
264 x 1   Pale Green
266 x 1   Mid Green
268 x 1   Dark Green
881 x 1   Peach
882 x 1   Dark Peach
883 x 1   Dull Pink
884 x 1   Brick Pink
896 x 1   Dark Pink
894 x 1   Mid Pink
895 x 1   Wine Pink
897 x 1   Wine
871 x 1   Mauve
872 x 2   Dark Mauve

CANVAS
8 holes per 2.5cm (1in)

QUANTITY
48 x 43cm (19 x 17in)

STITCH SIZE
8 stitches per 2.5cm (1in)

APPROXIMATE EMBROIDERED AREA
Approximately 43 x 38cm (17 x 15in)

Centre Front

Centre Front

Start Stitching

Chart for shells and seaweed sweater. The smallest shell is repeated on the back of the neck (see canvas placing diagrams)

	8040
	8042
	8044
	8046
	9306
	9202
	9264
	9508
	9510
	9600
	9640
	8330
	9620
	8510
	8512
	8546
	8548

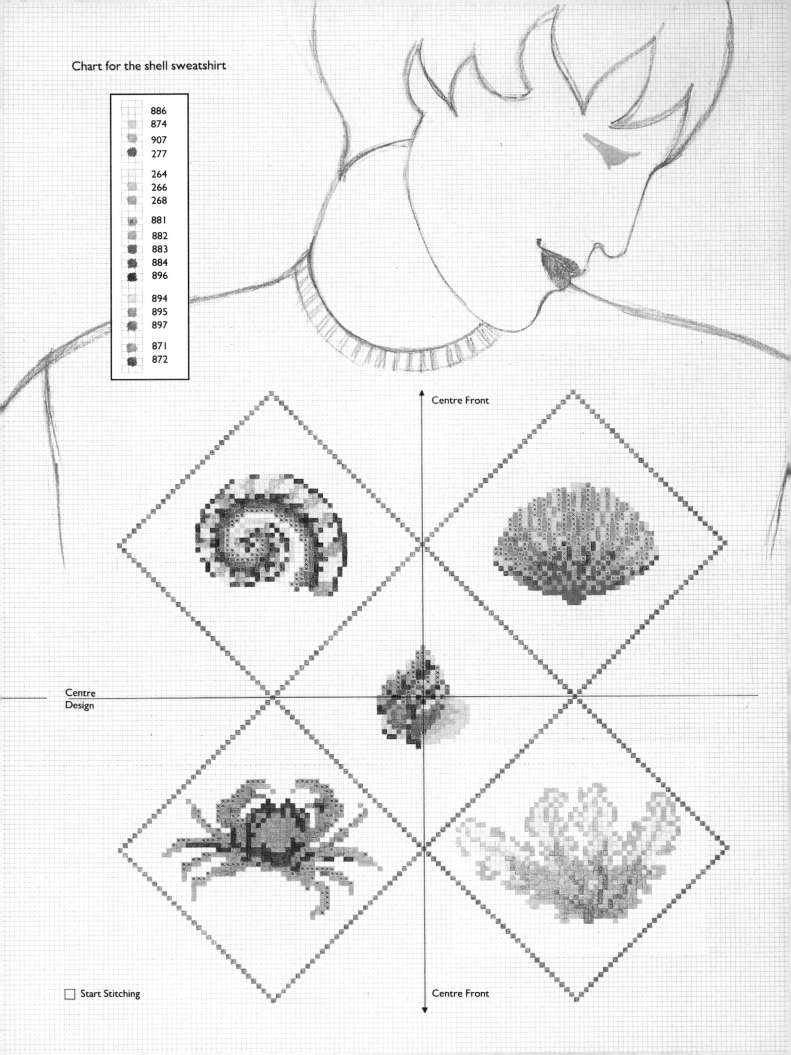

Chart for the shell sweatshirt

886
874
907
277

264
266
268

881
882
883
884
896

894
895
897

871
872

Centre Front

Centre
Design

Centre Front

□ Start Stitching

Shells could be made into a vertical banded design for a sweater

The back has
a bouquet of
flowers

FLORAL COLUMN JACKET

It is always fascinating to read the meaning of a design using the Victorians' 'language of flowers'. In this arrangement, the auriculas stand for 'painting'; the single rose for 'simplicity'; the violets denote 'humbleness', and the tulips 'pride'; the forget-me-nots 'lasting memories' and the convolvulus 'extinguished hopes'. However, the pink rose is for 'love' and the green leaves mean 'revived hope'.

The charts for the individual flowers came from many sources, and reflect the international popularity of Berlin woolwork. The rose and violet posy is American, the bow and convolvulus are from Berlin itself, whilst the tulip, single rose and top bunch of violets and forget-me-nots are French, as are the auriculas.

I have designed the columns to climb up the front of a long jacket and intertwine around the neck. Each flower has been singled out to form a 'spot' sampler pattern on a sweatshirt. There is also a large illustrated version of the back bunch of flowers from the main chart.

As you can see, there is a lot of intense work in this sumptuous design. Although it is not difficult, wait until you have fully mastered the technique and feel confident to undertake it.

GARMENT

Large long jacket of medium/heavy-weight knit, with T-shaped sleeves. The width at the button-band/armhole seam must measure 25cm at least (10in). If your garment is narrower, use a different gauge canvas to give a smaller embroidery (eg 7 or 8 stitches per 2.5cm/1in)

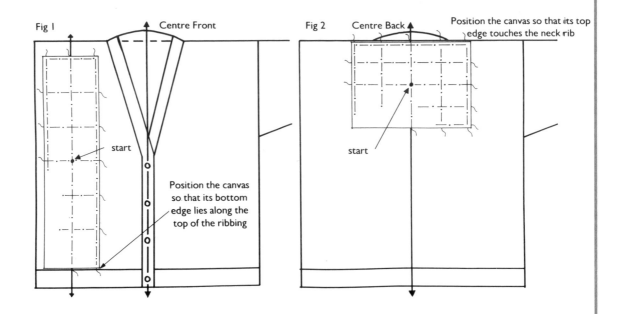

YARN
Anchor Tapestry Wool (Yarn)

NUMBER OF SKEINS

9002 x 2	Pale Green	
9004 x 2	Mid Green	
9022 x 2	Dark Green	
9618 x 2	Peach	
8348 x 1	Brick Pink	
9600 x 1	Terracotta	
8604 x 3	Pale Blue	
8608 x 2	Mid Blue	
8610 x 2	Dark Blue	
8588 x 2	Pale Mauve	
8590 x 2	Mid Mauve	
8592 x 1	Dark Mauve	
8504 x 1	Pale Pink	
8506 x 3	Mid Pink	
8508 x 2	Dark Pink	
8510 x 2	Very Dark Pink	
8040 x 3	Pale Yellow	
8042 x 3	Mid Yellow	
8044 x 2	Ochre	
9164 x 2	Lime Green	
9168 x 2	Sap Green	
9206 x 2	Olive Green	

8544 x 1	Pale Violet
8546 x 1	Mid Violet
8548 x 3	Dark Violet
8550 x 2	Very Dark Violet
8064 x 1	Gold
9302 x 1	Very Pale Green

CANVAS GAUGE
12 holes per 2.5cm (1in)

QUANTITY
Two pieces 74 x 24cm (29 x 9½in)
One piece 37 x 30.5cm (14½ x 12in)

STITCH SIZE
6 stitches per 2.5cm (1in)
(Embroider over every other hole)

EMBROIDERED AREA
Front: 69 x 19cm (27 x 7½in)
Back: 32 x 25.5cm (12½ x 10in)

This climbing and twining floral column is ▶
Berlin woolwork design at its most
sumptuous — and it makes a stunning jacket

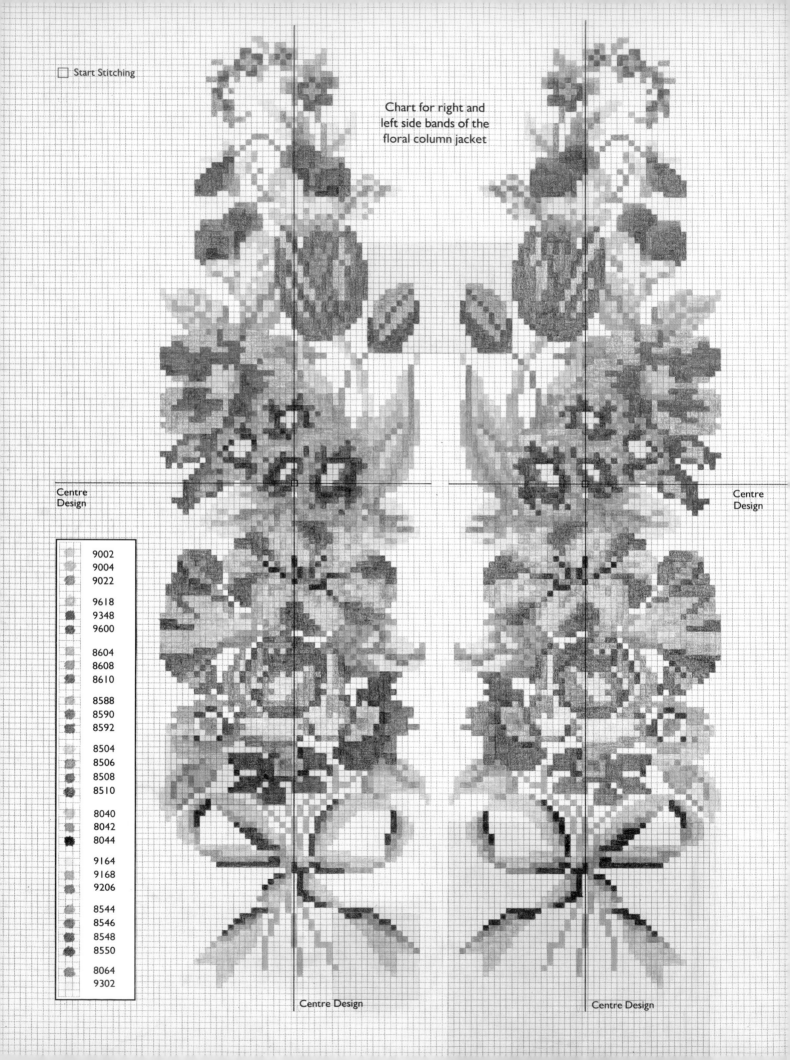

Start Stitching

Chart for right and
left side bands of the
floral column jacket

Centre
Design

Centre
Design

9002
9004
9022

9618
9348
9600

8604
8608
8610

8588
8590
8592

8504
8506
8508
8510

8040
8042
8044

9164
9168
9206

8544
8546
8548
8550

8064
9302

Centre Design

Centre Design

1 On both sides of the front of the jacket, measure along the shoulder seam from the neck band to the sleeve head. Mark halfway along each seam, then tack a vertical line down each side of the garment from this point to the bottom rib, as Fig 1.

2 Make sure that this line is straight by checking the measurement between it and the CF, at several points down the garment.

3 On the back of the garment, find and mark the CB line.

4 Mark and prepare all the pieces of canvas.

5 Fold each canvas lengthways and mark this line as well, to establish the centre points.

6 Position the front pieces as Fig 1, matching the centre line on the canvas with the tacked line on the garment. Pin and tack into place.

7 Make a grid of stitches across the canvas to secure it firmly and prevent slipping.

8 Position the back canvas as Fig 2. Pin and tack into place.

9 Make a grid of stitches as for front.

10 Working over every other hole of the canvas, start to embroider at the point shown on the chart in the middle of each canvas.

11 Finish as the Basic Instructions.

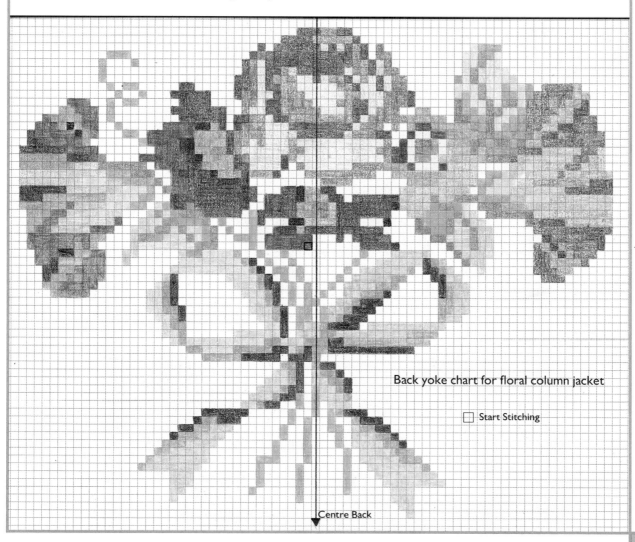

Back yoke chart for floral column jacket

☐ Start Stitching

Centre Back

The floral column back-yoke design could be stitched over a larger-gauge canvas, for a sweater or sweatshirt

FLORAL COLUMN SWEATSHIRT

GARMENT
Sweatshirt, or cotton round-neck sweater, fine/medium knit

YARN
Anchor Stranded Cotton (floss)
(Use all six strands; separate individual strands, then place together again before threading needle)

APPROXIMATE NUMBER OF SKEINS
202 x 1   Pale Green
204 x 1   Mid Green
205 x 1   Dark Green
336 x 1   Peach
337 x 1   Brick Pink
338 x 1   Terracotta
117 x 1   Pale Blue
118 x 1   Mid Blue
119 x 1   Dark Blue
108 x 1   Pale Mauve
109 x 1   Mid Mauve
111 x 1   Dark Mauve

893 x 1   Pale Pink
894 x 1   Mid Pink
895 x 1   Dark Pink
896 x 1   Very Dark Pink
305 x 1   Pale Yellow
306 x 1   Mid Yellow
307 x 1   Dark Yellow
308 x 1   Ochre
256 x 1   Lime Green
257 x 1   Sap Green
258 x 1   Olive Green
869 x 1   Pale Violet
870 x 1   Mid Violet
871 x 1   Dark Violet
872 x 1   Very Dark Violet
309 x 1   Gold

CANVAS GAUGE
8 holes per 2.5cm (1in)

QUANTITY
Approximately 43 x 38cm (17 x 15in)

STITCH SIZE
8 stitches per 2.5 (1in)

APPROXIMATE EMBROIDERED AREA
Approximately 38 x 33cm (15 x 13in)

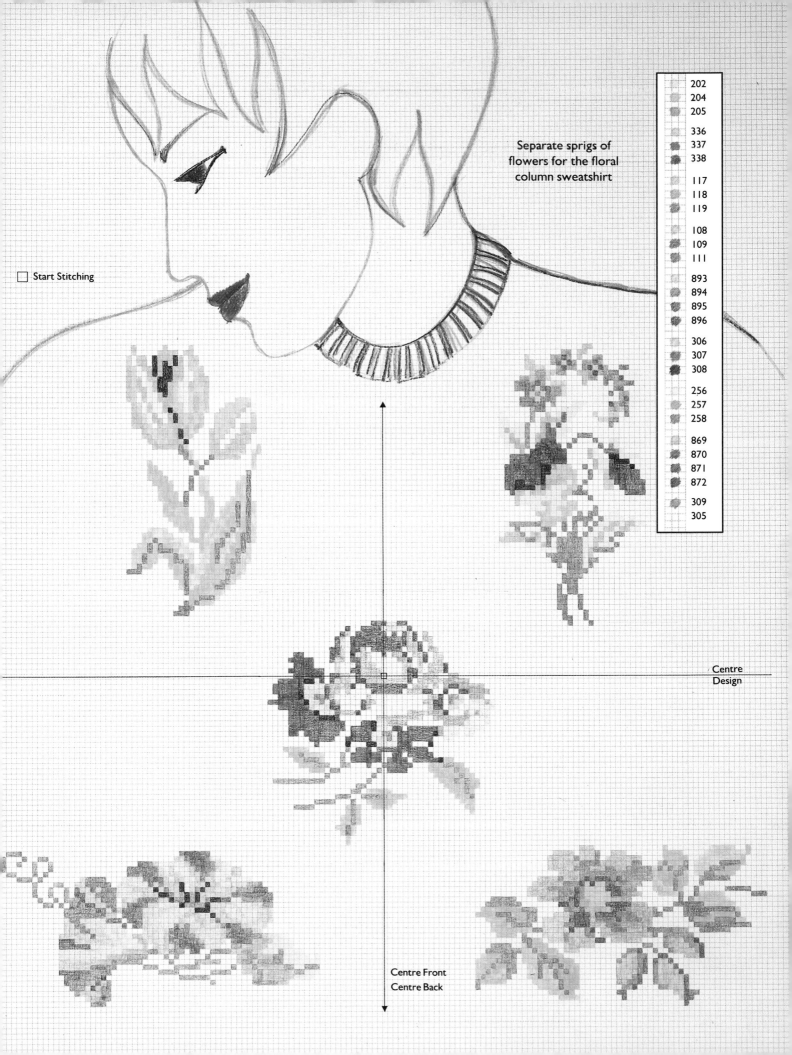

□ Start Stitching

Separate sprigs of
flowers for the floral
column sweatshirt

	202
	204
	205
	336
	337
	338
	117
	118
	119
	108
	109
	111
	893
	894
	895
	896
	306
	307
	308
	256
	257
	258
	869
	870
	871
	872
	309
	305

Centre
Design

Centre Front
Centre Back

BIBLIOGRAPHY

Bradley, Elizabeth DECORATIVE VICTORIAN NEEDLEWORK Ebury Press (1990)
Clabburn, Pamela BEADWORK Shire Publications (1980)
Colby, Averil (ed) SAMPLERS Batsford (1964)
de Dillmont, Therese ALBUM DE BRODERIES AU POINT DE CROIX DMC Library
  — ENCYCLOPEDIA OF NEEDLEWORK DMC Library
Fassett, Kaffe GLORIOUS NEEDLEPOINT Random Century (1987)
Kreuger, Glee A GALLERY OF AMERICAN SAMPLERS (THE THEODORE H.
  KAPNECK COLLECTION Bonanza Books (New York) (1978)
Modes & Travaux A SAMPLER OF ALPHABETS Sterling/Lark (1987)
Mueller, Heidi ROSEN, TULPEN, NELKEN . . . Museum fuer Deutsche Volkskunde, Berlin
Parker, Rosika THE SUBVERSIVE STITCH The Women's Press (1984)
Proctor, Molly G. VICTORIAN CANVAS WORK (BERLIN WOOLWORK) Batsford (1972)
Synge, Lanto ANTIQUE NEEDLEWORK Blandford Press (1982)
  — ROYAL SCHOOL OF NEEDLEWORK BOOK OF NEEDLEWORK AND
  EMBROIDERY The Oregon Press, Collins (1986)
Walton, Karin M. (ed) SAMPLERS IN THE CITY OF BRISTOL MUSEUM AND ART
  GALLERY Bristol Museum (1983)
Zischka, Ulrike STICKMUSTERTUECHER, Bilderheft der Staatlichen Museen, Preussisher
  Kulturbesitz, Berlin
THE EMBROIDERERS ALPHABET, DMC Library

STOCKISTS

DMC

UK DMC Creative World Ltd
Pullman Road
Wigston
Leicester LF8 2DY
(Yarns and Zweigart waste canvas)

USA DMC Corporation
Port Kearney Bld
#10 South Kearney
NJ 07032–0650

Australia DMC Needlecraft Pty
51–55 Carrington Road
PO Box 317
Earlswood 2206
New South Wales
(Yarns and Zweigart waste canvas)

USA Susan Bates Inc
30 Patewood Drive
Suite 35J
Greenville
SC 29615

Australia Coats Patons Crafts
Mulgrave
Victoria 3170

Canada Coats Patons Crafts
1001 Roselawn Avenue
Toronto
Ontario
M6D1B8

COATS/ANCHOR (COATS PATONS CRAFTS)

UK Coats Patons Crafts
(Customer Service Dept)
PO Box, McMullen Road
Darlington
Co Durham DL1 1YQ

Coates Paton Anchor
Mail Order Shop
Bedford Wool Shop
The Arcade
Bedford MK40 1MS
(Also Newey Water Soluble Pens)

CHARTWELL

H. W. Peel & Co Ltd
Greenford
Middlesex UB6 8BR
(Suppliers of Hobby Graph Paper)

ZWEIGART WASTE CANVAS (USA)

Joan Toggit
Weston Canal Plaza
2 Riverview Drive
Somerset
New Jersey 08873

ACKNOWLEDGEMENTS

First and foremost to Hilary Coe for her patience with my chaotic ways of working whilst she stitched, coloured the charts, collated and checked the information and eventually photographed these embroideries.

To Debbie Cripps for her cheerful moral support, sound practical advice and stitching for this book and for her work on all my other embroideries which, without her, would have ground to a halt.

To Helga Benson and Julia Hickman, embroiderers, who unselfishly lent me valued charts; especially Julia for her support and inspirational ideas for the book.

To Sarah Levitt, who, as assistant curator of Bristol City Museum & Art Gallery kindly gave her time and access to the Sampler Collection; Christine Stevens, Curator of Costume and Textiles at the Welsh Folk Museum for unearthing the Berlin Woolwork and charts; Sarah Hooper and Marie Husband at Coats Patons Crafts; Cara Ackerman at DMC Creative World Limited; Bill Brown at Chartwell, H. W. Peel & Company Limited, all of whom supplied me with materials to make this book.

Thanks also to the providers of the classic knitwear used throughout the book, Antony Sheppard of Machynlleth, Ludlow and Oxford for his 'Blue Stocking' range of sweaters and cardigans; Sue and Mike Holmewood of 'Holmewoods', Bristol, for all the other garments that have been embroidered; and not forgetting Betty Cripps for hand knitting.

To Vivienne Wells for giving me the opportunity to do this book and for all her calm good humoured advice and encouragement. Valerie Janitch for her amazing precision and clarity of thought when editing.

To Wendy and Roy Davies; Elizabeth Cecil; Binnie Collins, Ginny Spiegel and Jenny Whitaker; a big thank you for being so understanding and patient in waiting for your commissioned embroidered portraits until I completed this book.

I must thank here my friends and colleagues who rallied round with their various skills: Jenny Roberts, who undertook the difficult job of deciphering and typing my manuscript; Frank Phillips for the equally difficult job of deciphering the contract; Gill Sandford for being so understanding and organising my term's leave of absence from lecturing; Christopher Drew for just helping everywhere, but particularly the drizzling! And Hilary Jagger and Hazel Sutton for help with the last minute panic.

And lastly, my husband Stephen Jacobson, without whom this book would never have been completed.

CONVERSION CHARTS

WOOL

Anchor – DMC	Anchor – DMC	Anchor – DMC	Anchor – DMC
8256 – 7852	8220 – 7861	9790 – 7620	8740 – 7297
8212 – 7851	8938 – 7861	9792 – 7622	8506 – 7223
8204 – 7666	8922 – 7596	9796 – 7624	8508 – 7226
(7107)	8924 – 7327	9800 – 7309	8512 – 7266
8364 – 7193	8968 – 7542	(black)	8548 – 7895
8366 – 7194	8254 – 7122	8140 – 7767	8404 – 7208
8368 – 7195	9640 – 7466	8064 – 7508	9510 – 7144
(7217)	8634 – 7319	8546 – 7896	9666 – 7535
8352 – 7199	9540 – 7700	8596 – 7245	8136 – 7506
8488 – 7155	8304 – 7123	8400 – 7759	8348 – 7165
8490 – 7157	9020 – 7320	8504 – 7213	8042 – 7473
8522 – 7251	9022 – 7428	8508 – 7840	8044 – 7483
8588 – 7896	9008 – 7385	8202 – 7849	9602 – 7449
8590 – 7895	(7387)	8924 – 7925	8426 – 7115
8594 – 7708	9162 – 7549	8304 – 7175	8346 – 7951
8604 – 7241	9196 – 7583	9206 – 7377	9620 – 7949
8608 – 7241	9200 – 7364	9202 – 7393	9002 – 7369
8610 – 7243	8024 – 7474	9264 – 7359	9004 – 7370
8612 – 7247	8132 – 7914	8552 – 7268	8038 – 7472
8692 – 7797	8302 – 7122	9028 – 7389	8040 – 7504
8628 – 7314	8308 – 7124	(7408)	9164 – 7548
8630 – 7316	8310 – 7356	8164 – 7439	9168 – 7988
8814 – 7319	8330 – 7448	8046 – 7487	9302 – 7371
8624 – 7800	9526 – 7457	8018 – 7472	8052 – 7905
8626 – 7302	9540 – 7700	9508 – 7123	8482 – 7151
8822 – 7296	9564 – 7459	9600 – 7632	8484 – 7153
8914 – 7399	9642 – 7467	9306 – 7361	8486 – 7153
8918 – 7598	9788 – 7282	8048 – 7490	

COTTON

Anchor – DMC	Anchor – DMC	Anchor – DMC	Anchor – DMC
8 – 353	188 – 943	303 – 742	874 – 834
10 – 351	203 – 954	305 – 725	881 – 945
40 – 893	204 – 913	306 – 783	882 – 3064
46 – 666	205 – 912	307 – 783	884 – 400
74 – 605	218 – 890	308 – 782	886 – 3046
88 – 718	242 – 913	316 – 740	893 – 225
101 – 550	245 – 700	332 – 946	894 – 224
108 – 211	256 – 907	336 – 402	895 – 223
109 – 210	257 – 906	337 – 922	896 – 3721
110 – 209	258 – 904	338 – 921	897 – 221
111 – 208	264 – 3348	339 – 290	907 – 832
112 – 208	266 – 3347	365 – 435	925 – 970
117 – 794	268 – 3345	379 – 840	5975 – 356
118 – 793	278 – 472	387 – Ecru	277 – 830
119 – 333	281 – 580	410 – 995	803 – 967
121 – 794	298 – 972	869 – 3042	202 – 955
129 – 809	300 – 3078	870 – 3042	342 – 211
132 – 797	301 – 745	871 – 3041	
147 – 797	302 – 743	872 – 3041	

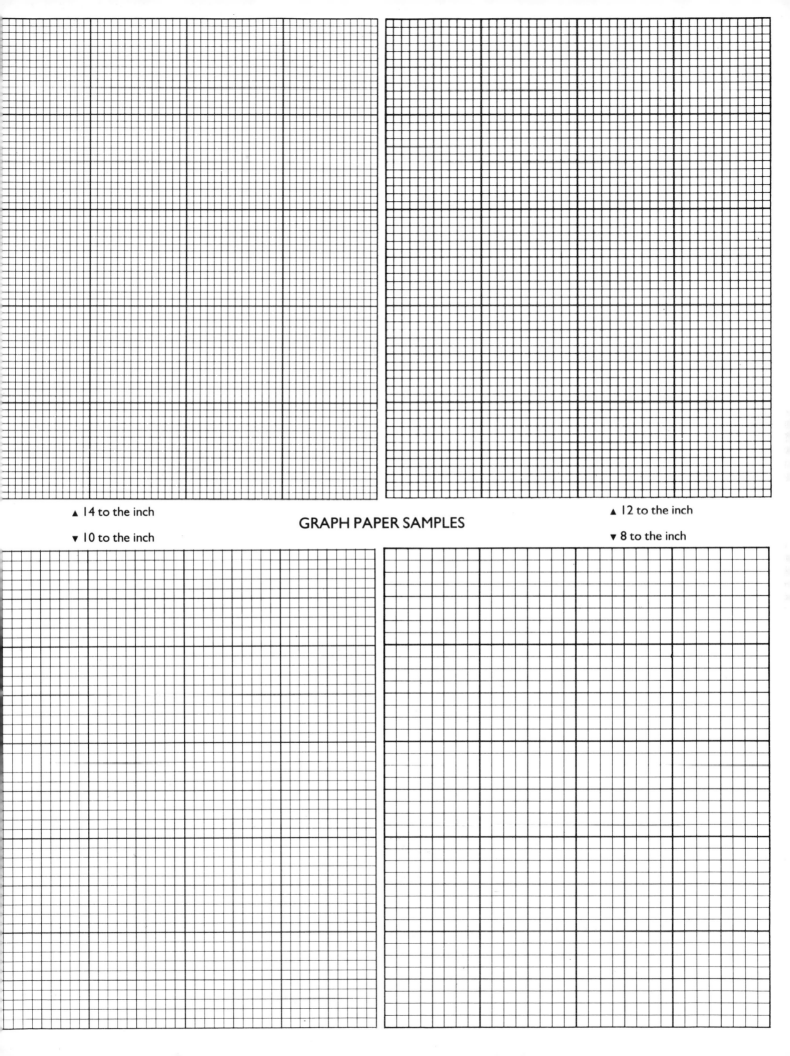

▲ 14 to the inch

▼ 10 to the inch

GRAPH PAPER SAMPLES

▲ 12 to the inch

▼ 8 to the inch

INDEX